GOING THROUGH THE FIRE

DEVELOPING A FAITH THAT PERSEVERES

By

David A. Treat

ISBN: 1-4107-8433-9 (e-book)
ISBN: 1-4107-8432-0 (Paperback)

This book is printed on acid free paper.

1stBooks – rev.10/09 /03

This book is dedicated to my wife, whose strength, courage and faith have always been an inspiration to me.

Table of Contents

Forward

Thanksgiving 1993. As with all Thanksgivings, it was a time for family; a time for friends; a time for re-connection; a time for love.

Still basking in the warmth of their family reunion, the Treat family, David, Marcia and three of their children, were on their way home to Phoenix, Arizona, when the unthinkable happened…a tragic car accident that would not only change all of their lives forever, but would test their faith as well.

Post Thanksgiving 1993. A time of tragedy; a time of trials; a time of physical and emotional toughness; a time of fear, doubt, anxiety and worry. And yet…it was a time of blessings…many rich and bountiful blessings.

Going Through The Fire is an amazing account of one man's faith…faith in his family, faith in his friends and faith in God.

Going Through The Fire is also a love story. It will inspire you to love your spouse and children more and to love God more.

Every word that David Treat has written caused me to examine my own life.

Could I be doing more as a husband and father?

Could I be spending more time with my wife and children?

Could I hug more, laugh more, play more?

As a child of God, could I be in higher service to humanity?

While David's accident may have been tragic, his re-telling of the events since 1993 is a triumph.

Going Through The Fire will enhance your faith in your family and friends; empower you to believe in yourself even more; and be in high celebration of the Glory of God!

I encourage all of our sixty-five million readers of *Chicken Soup For The Soul* to read *Going Through The Fire* and to give at least one copy to someone they love.

May the Blessings continue...

Barry Spilchuk
Co-author: A *Cup Of Chicken Soup For The Soul*
Founder "Let's Talk...", a company dedicated to bringing families closer.

Preface

It was early morning in May 2000. Jeff Treat (Dave's sixteen-year-old son) and I filled our canteens in preparation for leaving Phantom Ranch, a camping area at the bottom of the Grand Canyon. I wanted to get on the trail before it got too hot. I was in my usual hurry-up mode. As we started to leave, Jeff said, "Let's sit down and pray first." I wish Dave could have witnessed this. It was refreshing to see a sixteen-year-old young man put his trust with the Lord. Hearing Jeff asking to sit down and pray, I thought about the great job Dave and Marcia have done raising their kids. How faithful God has been to them.

I was mowing the lawn when my wife, Diane, motioned for me to come into the house. She had just learned from a telephone call that the Treats were in a car accident. It was bad—Dave was paralyzed and Marcia might not even survive. I was stunned. Dave and I were friends. For years our families had attended the same Baptist church. We attended Sunday school and Wednesday night bible classes together. We played on the church softball team. We were both lawyers. I had referred cases to Dave and even tried a case against him in Superior Court. Diane knew that I was supposed to go to Utah.

The next morning I flew to Provo with Pastor Norm. When I walked into Dave's room, I saw he was in a halo (a circular brace that screws into the skull to keep the neck stable). He was lying in a bed that rotated from side to side. He was awake, but could not talk. There were all kinds of medical devices attached to him. He looked up and gave me a great big smile. I wondered how a man who is paralyzed from the neck down and whose wife is in a coma could give me a smile. But he did. Another quadriplegic friend of mine says that when tragedy happens you have a choice. You can get bitter or you can get better. From this moment I knew Dave was going to have a hard life ahead of him—but he was going to get better.

Marcia looked even worse than Dave. Her head was swollen and she had a huge black eye. There were so many tubes going in and out of her that she looked like she was at the bottom of a spaghetti bowl. I asked one of the nurses if Marcia was going to make it. The nurse turned from me and started to cry. I called home to my wife and told her the gravity of Dave and Marcia's conditions. It was hard for me to have faith that Marcia was going to survive. Diane told me that God had given her a scripture—God's arm was not so short that it could not reach out and heal!

I don't know why bad things happen to good people. I do know that God has said His grace is sufficient and that His strength is made perfect in my weakness, so that when I am weak, I am strong. *Going Through The Fire* is proof that this is true for the Treats. Dave cannot reach out and shake your hand, but his smile will grip and greet you like no handshake ever could. He cannot physically hug his family or his friends, but his words touch our hearts.

Long before this tragedy struck, the Treats built their house upon God and his principles for living. The Bible says of such a house: "the rain descended, and the floods came, and the winds blew, and burst against the house, and yet it did not fall, for it had been founded upon the rock." (Mt 7:25)

Bud Roberts

Message From The Author

For a number of years, friends and family had encouraged me to write about my emotions and feelings since my life-changing accident. I kept pushing the idea aside. I knew there was a lot of pain buried inside of me from my life since the accident. I wasn't ready to revisit my pain. I didn't think I would ever be ready.

I wrote a condensed form of "David and Marcia" several years ago. It is a love story about how my wife and I met and our life together before the accident. I wrote these pages so my children would know a little more about their parents. Recently, after reading "David and Marcia", I realized the story was not complete. I resolved to write what I had put off for years. I was finally ready. The story was ready to be written down.

I wondered if I still remembered enough to communicate my emotions and feelings from as far back as seven and one-half years. I have read that every experience we ever have is stored in the memory banks in our mind. Whether or not this is true, I know that once I started to write, the words began to flow freely as feelings filled my being with power that surprised me. Emotionally, it was difficult to write some of these pages, but I believe it was therapeutic. My mind has been released.

While writing *Going Through The Fire* I called it simply, *My Story,* because I was very aware that it was told from my perspective about events as I perceived them. My wife and each of my children entered different fires. Like "David and Marcia", *Going Through The Fire* was initially written for my children and a few close friends.

I am deeply indebted to my daughter-in-law, Erica Treat, who spent many hours editing my manuscript.

David A. Treat—September 2001

Going Through The Fire

DEVELOPING A FAITH THAT PERSEVERES

Consider it pure joy, my brothers, whenever you face trials of many kinds, because you know that the testing of your faith develops perseverance. Perseverance must finish its work so that you may be mature and complete, not lacking anything.

James 1:2-4

Introduction

My family had visited my sister's family in Sandy, Utah over Thanksgiving. Now Marcia and I, with our three youngest children, Alana (age 18), Kevin (age 15) and Jeffrey (age 10) are traveling toward our home in Phoenix. We have much of a long day's drive still ahead of us. Alana is at the wheel, driving along a two-lane highway outside of Kanab, Utah. As I half doze in the rear seat, I suddenly notice the car is drifting

1

dangerously close to the right edge of the highway. "Hey, watch i—!" I call out. The "t" of "it" dies on my lips as my mind goes blank. Our minivan has swerved off the highway, skidded and then rolled three times before coming to rest.

When I awaken, I immediately realize I can't move my arms or legs. I want to call to someone, but I can't speak. A numbing fear grips me as I realize I am on a vent. My older sister was hospitalized, totally paralyzed and on a vent for six years before she mercifully died a few years ago. I always considered her existence in the hospital, unable to move or speak for six long years, a cruel living hell. Now I am in a hospital, unable to move or speak, and on a vent! It is too horrible to believe real! Surely this is just a dream—a nightmare! But it seems so terribly real!

A nurse comes to me and asks if I would like to see my family. Seeing my weak attempt at a nod (my neck is braced), she disappears and within a few minutes I find myself surrounded by my children. My spirits lift on seeing them, unhurt and talking cheerfully. They sing praise songs which I enjoy very much. I am told I have a broken neck and am paralyzed from the neck down. Marcia has a serious brain injury and is in a coma. I hear the words they speak, but it is more than I can take in. After a short visit everyone leaves and I go to sleep.

This accident transformed my world. It took me from my secure, orderly life, with a loving family and God, to the edge of insecurity, chaos and despair. In the pages that follow I tell of my journey, the people who helped me along the way and especially of my feelings—physical, emotional and spiritual—as I slowly found my way back home. I begin with a few pages about my life with Marcia before the accident.

David A. Treat

Part I: David and Marcia

David A. Treat

We Meet

My first college summer I worked at Motorola and made good money which was socked away for school. Looking back, it seems a little crazy that the next summer I worked for fifty dollars each month. I had been hired to be on the student staff at the National Assembly Grounds for the American Baptists, which is located on the shore of Green Lake in Wisconsin. I was about to embark on a summer that would change my life.

I went to work at the National Assembly Grounds for the American Baptists (which is called "Green Lake") because of the adventure it promised. Marcia went because she lived only a few hundred miles away and had been a camper with her church group at Green Lake several times in high school. I believe God had His hand on each of us, directing our courses across thousands of miles to bring us together in His own time.

7

"I'm going sailing after lunch. Would anyone like to come with me?" My question seemed to be directed at all fifteen of the student staffers who shared my table as we ate our lunch, shoulder-to-shoulder, in the small staff dining room. But there was really only one voice I was listening for.

"I would," Marcia's voice chimed out from down and across the table. My heart leaped. I had been hesitant (shy me!) to ask Marcia out directly. Now I had a date. Incredible!

After lunch, as Marcia and I walked down to the waterfront, I sweated out every step. I had said I was going sailing because it sounded like something that might entice someone (maybe Marcia) to come with me. But I knew my sailing skills were next to none and the lake was large enough for us to get lost forever. I breathed a tremendous sigh of relief when we were told the only sailboat was already on the lake. We would have to settle for a rowboat. Rowing around the lake was great fun and I even had her row to the dock area when we ended our outing, so everyone would think she rowed me around the lake. As we walked back toward our dorms, I slipped a very tentative arm around Marcia's waist. Immediately I felt her arm firmly around my waist. With a thrill I realized, "This girl likes me as much as I like her. YES!!!"

We Court

Green Lake is a huge, lakeside resort that includes a large hotel, world-class golf course, waterfront and numerous smaller buildings. It is spread over several square miles of beautiful hardwood forest carved with miles of quiet, winding roads.

Almost every evening the 110 college kids who made up the student staff had a party (Marcia and I organized a T-shirt tie dying party), a film projector movie (no VCRs yet), or some of us piled into cars and went to a pizza parlor in a small town two miles down the highway. Every afternoon, between lunch and dinner, Marcia and I swam in the lake and napped in the grass. We went for long walks together along the quiet roadways and at night we even walked across the golf course (our favorite). From morning at 6:30 a.m. when we walked down to work (I was a

9

busboy, she was a waitress on another team), until we went to bed, usually around 1:00 a.m., Marcia and I were inseparable. I had really fallen hard for this girl.

At the end of the summer I accompanied Marcia to her home in Cleveland, Ohio. I had already met Marcia's parents. They had come to Green Lake for a weekend to be with Marcia (and probably to check out the nutty redhead she told them about in her letters). We hoped to convince them to let Marcia transfer to the University of Arizona, where I attended. Marcia went to a small university in Ohio and was very unsure her parents would consider a transfer all the way to Arizona. Marcia and I decided she should ask to transfer for the second semester because it seemed impossible to transfer for the first semester, which started in ten days. To our amazement, her parents suggested trying to get Marcia admitted to U of A immediately. Many years later I learned they agreed to send their daughter to a school two thousand miles away, where she knew only me and I was a boy they had just met, because she "glowed when she was around me." One week later I met Marcia at the airport in Tucson and we were together again.

At Green Lake Marcia and I had long talk-walks nearly every day. Within the first two weeks of being together we talked about the qualities we felt were important in a marriage partner. I knew she was the right one for me. I thought love at first sight happened only in Hollywood…until I met Marcia. Now that she was at U of A, I knew we would be together forever.

My roommate and I struck a deal with Marcia: if she would cook dinner, we would let her eat free (such a deal!). We ate together nearly every night and I found she was quite a cook. After dinner we usually studied until I walked her to her dorm at 11:00 p.m. She slept at her dorm and went to classes during the day. Every afternoon and evening we were together.

My tiny rental was infested with roaches and the kitchen was especially bad. Marcia loathed roaches. One night, after encountering a number of the insects, she couldn't take it anymore. She decided she would, once and for all, RID MY KITCHEN OF ROACHES! Getting a can of bug spray, she started spraying the baseboards and crevices of the tiny kitchen. In about thirty seconds they started coming out—by the hundreds! I heard Marcia screaming and came running. Finding the floor of the kitchen awash with the crazed beasts, I threw open the back door and began sweeping them outside by the broomfuls. Thankfully, this occurred after dinner.

We had a great college group at church. We were all poor and many of us were in love. Our church wasn't strong in teaching the Bible, but we didn't know what we were missing. We had our friends and for now, that was enough.

In February, Marcia and I secretly began planning our wedding for the upcoming Christmas vacation. I was stocking groceries part-time, taking home a whopping $235 each month. Marcia hoped to work at least a few hours each week too. Putting our heads together, we worked out a budget within our means. When Marcia's parents visited at Spring break we announced our engagement. Of course our parents tried to convince us to wait until we had finished school, but we wouldn't hear of it. We were young and in love. So plans for the wedding began.

Marcia did something special to me. I was a stronger, more confident person because of her. If someone so special loved me, believed in me, then I must be special too. I walked a little, no, a lot taller knowing Marcia was at my side. Marcia did even more than this for me. She was a strong friend. We talked about everything together. We shared our dreams, our insecurities, our disappointments, our victories—we shared our lives. I had never before experienced such a strong bond. I thrived on it!

We Build Our Lives Together
As Students

After a two-day honeymoon we were back in Tucson, but there was a problem. The studio apartment we were getting through married housing (seventy-eight dollars/mo—a huge bargain even in 1972!) wouldn't be available until January 15th. Fortunately, our very good friends, Tina and Lee Fogleman (who had been married only four months), offered to share their tiny, two-bedroom house with us. It was loads of fun to live with Tina and Lee, but the tight quarters brought on extra tension for newlyweds. We were very excited and somewhat relieved, when it was finally time to move to our own place.

Furnishing our studio apartment on our meager budget was a challenge that we took up with enthusiasm. We splurged on a seventy-five dollar stereo. That thirty-five dollar recliner from

13

Joe's basement was a steal! I built our entertainment center with decorative cement blocks, together with long boards that I antiqued. It was our happy abode, and we loved it.

In our cozy, one room apartment, life was not always *oozing* with love. When Marcia got angry, she came at me, fired off a salvo of cheap shots (my opinion) and then stalked quickly away without allowing me to respond. Of course I confronted her with the unfairness of this way to fight, but she had gotten away with it for years and found it an extremely difficult practice to break (that means she kept doing it for several years!).

Two days after we had a fight she would bring it up again. I had forgotten all about it and couldn't understand why she had to put it before us. "But we haven't resolved our anger yet," she insisted. I couldn't even remember what we had argued about, but *she* could. Painstakingly, we talked through the two-day-old argument and apologies were made. I didn't like doing this. It seemed unnecessary to me, but oh-so-important to Marcia. It took me several years to appreciate the importance of Marcia's way.

We knew these behaviors of each other before we were married—they just didn't come up as often and didn't dominate so much of our lives. Forging the emotional bonds necessary for a strong marriage doesn't come without pain. If only I could remember to close the lid of the toilet!

I had my heart set on going to medical school. The Lord's plan called for me to be an attorney. It's a humbling experience to oppose the Lord. So, after being denied acceptance to medical school and wondering for a year what career field I should pursue, I entered a toxicology program at the university. But my heart was not in it. It was hard for me to give up the thought of being a doctor.

I began studying toxicology in 1973, when our country was in the throws of President Nixon's Watergate coverup. Nearly all of the President's top advisers were eventually convicted of serious criminal acts. And nearly all were attorneys! My first thoughts of going to law school occurred while watching the Watergate hearings. It seemed our country needed more lawyers with strong moral character. I wanted to be that kind of lawyer, but I heard it was as hard to get into law school as medical school. Marcia and I didn't raise our hopes too high and we didn't tell anyone about my law school aspirations. When the acceptance letter came we were ecstatic. There was more excitement to come. When I told the law school about my financial situation (I had no money in savings), I was given a full tuition scholarship. I felt not only accepted, but also wanted. It was a good, warm feeling after my cool rejection by medical school.

Six weeks before law school was to begin, I quit my fulltime summer job stocking groceries to vacation with Marcia for five weeks in the Volkswagen van we had purchased new, a year earlier. We had no definite time schedule, but planned to spend time in the Canadian Rockies before traveling across southern Canada to reenter the U.S in North Dakota. Marcia's grandparents in Springfield, Illinois, my brother's family in Wilmington, Delaware and Marcia's parents in Cleveland, Ohio were also part of our itinerary. We did all this and even more, finding time to spend a night with Marcia's brother in Haverford, Pennsylvania and have a day in Washington D.C., where we lunched with a good friend from Green Lake. We camped in our van and cooked on a Coleman stove for the first part of our travels, but we loaded up bedroom furniture at Marcia's parent's house (for a small home we were able to rent) and camped in a pup tent on the way home. It was the perfect vacation for the tough, lean years that were to follow.

Marcia's menstrual period had always been irregular. Sometimes she went a year or more without a period. Her doctors informed us she might not be able to conceive and that her chances were much greater in her early twenties than later in life. We had previously not planned to have children until I finished law school. But now we decided to go off birth control right away.

Six months later Marcia met me as I came out of the law school. Without speaking, she handed me a transparent plastic cup sealed on top with transparent tape. In it was a single pink rosebud. I was at a loss as I stared blankly at the cup. Then it hit me. Marcia had planned to have a pregnancy test that morning. I clutched her to me and we hugged and kissed each other. We would be parents after all!

I worked my way through law school doing legal clerking (research and drafting documents) for several small law firms. During my undergraduate years money had always been scarce. Now that I was in law school, finding money for bare survival seemed harder than ever. Sometimes it was several weeks into the semester before I could even afford books for all of my law classes. All class books were on reserve in the law library, but I had to work as much as possible during the day and I hated to make the three-mile trip to campus after dinner to study.

Marcia and I remained tightly bound to our college friends and we hung out with them regularly. When Alana was born, she went everywhere with us because *babysitters cost money*. "Someday we may be tempted to recall

17

these days as our best times together," I said to Marcia. "Well they're not! If we had a hundred dollars more money each month, they might be." My income varied greatly depending on how much work was available from the several firms that gave me assignments. Too often I was writing checks to pay bills, when I had no money in my account, hoping I would collect some money the next day. Somehow the power never got turned off and even though we were late on rent, our landlord was understanding. The Lord was teaching us to walk by faith in our finances. It's easy to talk, but not easy to walk.

I hold my breath as I search for my number on the page showing who passed the bar exam. The numbers have just been posted on the bulletin board and the area is crowded with my classmates and others who are anxiously searching as well. There are so many numbers…but wait, there it is! I passed, my God, I passed. The tension in my body visibly releases. Later I learn that only 49% passed. Marcia and I celebrate. We are off to Phoenix to set up my law practice!

Our Love For Each Other
And For God Grows

Our new church, Madison Baptist, provided us with Bible preaching and instruction that I had missed for many years and Marcia had never experienced. She thought a Christian was someone who went to church! We began getting involved in youth ministry where we felt the Lord was calling us. Praying together became a regular part of our lives.

Building a law practice takes time. I initially had very few clients or cases, so money was still extremely scarce. Fortunately, I typed very well and secretly acted as my own secretary. We were getting better at walking by faith in our finances. When Kevin was born, our two-bedroom apartment suddenly seemed very small.

"I'd like to have you show me some houses," Marcia said over the telephone to Mo, a female real estate agent.

"What price range are you interested in?" asked Mo.

"I'm not sure," replied Marcia.

"Well, how much do you have for a down payment?" questioned Mo.

"Nothing," Marcia answered. Marcia quickly explained, "When we find the right house, God will provide the money." There was a distinct pause as Mo digested this information.

We made a believer out of Mo. Three weeks later we fell in love with the house on Sharon Avenue, where we currently live. A few days after being shown the house I unexpectedly settled the largest case of my two-year-old legal career. I had been working on this case for over a year. My fee was $8,500—exactly what I needed to close escrow on the house. I didn't earn a fee this large again for several years. The home was titled in our names, but we never forgot that it was God's house.

Early in our relationship Marcia and I had discussed the importance of a mother being at home with her children. Even though Marcia had a college degree, when Alana was born Marcia had not continued employment outside the home. I drove an older model car, we didn't go out to dinner often and Marcia found ways to make a chicken go for three meals. But now, with the purchase of a house, we found our mortgage payment was much more than our apartment rent. Suddenly, payments of all kinds were being made late. When the house mortgage got behind two and one-half months and we received a notice that foreclosure would soon begin, we did some hard praying and a little questioning. Should Marcia get a job? Would God take away what He had given? Our legs of faith were turning to jelly. Somehow, God always had an interesting way of bringing clients to me, or settling cases in a timely way. I can smile now, but it was not easy going through the financial fire of the first years of my law practice. Even then, God was making us strong and building our faith.

In college I had wanted to be a doctor. Now I thanked God for saying "no" to that prayer. My law practice proved ideal for arranging time to be with my children. After all, I was my own boss! If I wanted to take off every Tuesday afternoon at 3:00, so I could be with six-year-old Alana at Yamaha Music School, I could do it. I did this and much more. I had the perfect job!

Law can easily become a workaholic profession, but I knew my priorities must be first God, and second family. I was determined that my work, which I loved very much, and other interests, would not take my life out of balance with God or my family. Marcia was a strong encourager in making sure I kept my priorities right. She demanded her own time with me!

When Marcia became pregnant with our third child, we decided to have a midwife delivery so that the child could be born in the comfort of our own bedroom. Late in Marcia's pregnancy, after getting home from church on a Sunday evening, she told me she was having small, regular contractions. We put Alana (7 years) and Kevin (4 years) to bed without a word of this. The contractions continued to increase in strength and to come closer together. Soon it was time to telephone Marilyn, our nurse-midwife, who agreed she should come right away. As with Alana and Kevin, we used Lamaze methods for relaxation so that Marcia could deliver the baby without need of medication. Marcia was fantastic (I was a terrific coach, too!) and our little baby boy was born at 12:37 Monday morning.

The commotion in our room following baby Jeffrey's birth woke Kevin and he came into our room rubbing his eyes. "Kevin," I said, "come see your new baby brother." Upon seeing the baby, Kevin's eyes popped wide open and he exclaimed, "I'm going to tell Alana!" Soon both children were in our room and each wanted several turns holding the baby. Finally I got the children settled back into bed and Marcia and I bedded down with our new baby between us. I had started to doze off when I heard a gentle rapping at the bedroom door and two small voices saying, "We want to hold our baby brother again." Both children had one more round of holding the baby and then everyone went to bed for good. It was a very special night of family bonding.

We had three children and felt our family was complete. But six years later we found that, once again, our plan was not the same as God's plan for us.

I decided to ask Eddie, a new high schooler at church, to help me coach Kevin's farm level Little League team. As we got to know each other, Eddie began hanging out with my family more and more. Eddie had never known his biological father. His mother and stepfather were divorced and Eddie lived with his stepfather. He didn't talk much about his life at home, but Marcia and I suspected it was not good.

In June, Eddie (age 16) came to us with some difficult news. His stepfather had kicked him out of the house and his mother could not take him in. Eddie had nowhere to go. My family had grown very close to Eddie. We held a short family counsel. After talking for only a few minutes it was clear my children were eager to have Eddie move in with us. The thought of Eddie joining our family also excited Marcia and me. There was one problem: our house had only three bedrooms. For Eddie to stay with us, he would have to share Kevin and Jeffrey's small bedroom. Kevin (age 10) and Jeffrey (age 6) quickly agreed to this. I told Eddie that he could live with us on condition that he would be as one of my children. We would love and provide for him; he would be subject to our authority. And so it came to be that Marcia and I got a fourth child, my three children got a big brother and Eddie got a new family.

Eddie was a lot of fun to have in our family. He brought a new level of humor to our mealtimes. But Eddie wasn't used to being accountable to anyone and this was especially true as to where he was going or when he would be home. It was a tall order for Marcia and me to know how to parent a teenager who had grown up in a dysfunctional family, where accountability had never been required. It was tougher still for Eddie to adjust to a new family, with many new demands, while being crammed into a small bedroom with two younger brothers. There were a number of problems at first, but through it all Marcia and I clung to the firm belief that Eddie was a gift from God and God doesn't make mistakes. We spent more time praying for wisdom in parenting Eddie and for Eddie, himself, than for our three other children combined. Somehow we all got through the tough periods and in time, Eddie became, in fact, my son.

Marcia and I found a strong ministry teaching Sunday school, counseling church camps and going on youth trips. Marcia had a gift at counseling. She was a favorite among the junior and senior high kids. For over a year we were in charge of the entire junior high program, including Sunday mornings, evenings and trips. It was a calling with tremendous rewards, and it was plain fun.

I grew up in a family that ate breakfast and dinner together seven days a week. Early on, I made this practice a priority for my own family. I had experienced that there is something special that happens at mealtime beyond consumption of food. I saw that children and parents who came together at mealtime became strongly bonded families. My daughter caught this "magic of mealtime" in our family perfectly in a short high school essay, set out below. She also captured our family chemistry with a witty style all her own. (Alana was age 16 when she wrote this essay, Kevin was age 13 and Jeffrey was age 9.)

Have you ever noticed how the simplest things in life can bring enjoyment and laughter? Take, for instance, my family around the dinner table for the evening meal. Sounds rather normal and healthy, doesn't it? However, lurking beneath the mask of innocence lies a comedy routine that would put any onlooker in stitches.

Let me set the scene for you. It's the end of an uneventful day in the world. We're tired of the daily routine and want to let our hair down. Fortunately, the easiest and most enjoyable exercise to rid us of our boredom is laughter, however, our targets are usually one another. Thankfully, through the years of continuous teasing, we've all learned to chuckle at our own mistakes and shortcomings. Why not? It's something we all have in common, humanness—except for my little brother!

Now let me introduce you to the people with whom I share my food, washing machine, hair blower and laugh lines. First, there is my father. He's naturally easy going, responsible, and loving, however, he is slowly, but very surely, becoming deaf, forgetful, and absent minded. When giving him instructions, we must be sure to have him read our lips and repeat them back to us every few minutes to insure their completion. In fact, just today he totally forgot to pick up my oldest brother from his work. As of this minute, I know not the whereabouts of my dearly loved sibling. I assure you this will be a largely exaggerated issue to be discussed in future days.

Next, there is my mother, the queen of profound statements. While we're engaging in a meal, there's no telling when good ol' Mom will interrupt saying, "It rained today," or, "Kevin is 13 years old." Keep in mind that these statements are not related to any previous conversations. They simply seem to appear out of nowhere. Occasionally we'll mumble, "Good observation Mom!" or, "You don't say! How ever did you come to that conclusion?" But usually we just smile and agree, leaving her to ponder her new discovery.

Thirdly, is the older of my two little brothers, Kevin. Now, he seems harmless enough at first; but don't be fooled. Never, under any circumstances, put yourself in the position that requires you to disagree, debate or argue with him. The rapture will come before he gives in and admits he's wrong. If I come to the table wearing a red shirt, given the chance, he will argue intently that my shirt is green. He has the art of questioning and calmly rationalizing until I've dug my own grave. By then I'm at the point of no return. He'll leave me doubting my sanity and wondering if my shirt isn't green after all.

Lastly, is my youngest brother, Jeffrey. You see, Jeffrey seems to have a song for everything. If he doesn't know one, he'll make it up. Familiar tunes from hymns, choruses, and commercials take on new meaning when he hears a catchy phrase. Whether or not he knows the meaning of what he's singing is not a priority. As long as it's his voice he hears, it's music to his ears.

Now, you're probably wondering where I fit in among all these activities. In between bites, I tend to make the rounds from loved one to loved one. When I'm not arguing with Kevin, I'm singing with Jeffrey. While Dad's trying to remember the joke I told him the night before, I ask Mom if she's had any new revelations. All in all, it's our way of sharing together things no one besides our family could love us for. I'm convinced that's why God gave them to us in the first place.By the way, would you care to come for dinner sometime? We'd love to have you!

Eddie was 19 years old and had moved from our residence when the above essay was written. I feel sure Alana would have hailed him as the mealtime entertainer because he kept us laughing at dinner. Seeing the way my children cared for each other, one of Kevin's friends dubbed us the "Beaver Cleaver" family. I took this as a very high compliment.

When my parents had their 50th wedding anniversary, during the summer of 1991, Marcia and I organized a family reunion. Renting a cabin in Payson for four days, we squeezed nine adults and ten of my parents' grandchildren inside (only Eddie didn't make the trip). Marcia and I slept in the loft with all the kids, including three of our own. We had lots of long talks with the kids and we sang praise songs together nearly every night. We were in our element, and we had the time of our lives.

Eddie had a younger half brother, Jason, who was forbidden by his father (Eddie's stepfather) to have contact with Eddie or my family after Eddie came to live with us. But in early 1990, Jason's parents separated with Jason living with his mother, who welcomed contact with my family. Jason began hanging out with us regularly and we grew very close. Tragically, in May 1992, Jason's mother was killed in an accident with a drunk driver. Jason's father had not communicated with Jason since his parent's separation and so Jason (age 16) moved in with us during this very painful time in his life. One year later, Jason and his father mended their relationship and he returned to live with him. It was with great reluctance that I saw him leave, because I knew he was not returning to a good environment. But I was thankful for the year he spent with us as we provided a bridge to sustain him after his mother's death until relations could be revived with his father.

The bond between Marcia and I had grown stronger than I ever knew was possible. We prayed together, loved together and labored together. We were seeing the fruits of this togetherness in our family and our ministries. It was very satisfying. During this time I remarked to Marcia, "These are our best years."

In November 1993 my family spent Thanksgiving with my sister Cindy's family in Sandy, Utah. On the way home we had the accident that changed the course of our lives.

Part II: Going Through The Fire

David A. Treat

31 Days In Provo

I cannot speak, but I can communicate as my children hold up an alphabet board so I can indicate letters to slowly spell out words. One thing I spell out right away, "Take me off the vent or let me die." I will not live for years lying in a hospital bed, unable to move or speak, waiting to die. I will not go through the living hell my sister endured.

My cervical injury is very high and my doctor does not believe I can breathe without the vent (I learn this later). Nevertheless, he agrees to remove the vent tube at my insistence to see how I do. Surprising everyone but myself, I *am* able to breathe on my own—praise God!—but my breathing is very shallow and barely sustains me.

"How much movement can I expect to get back as I recover," I ask Dr. Gaufin.

"You're there," he replies.

Several seconds go by as his response sinks in. Dr. Gaufin is explaining that the spinal cord swelling cut off the blood supply to the nerve and that once nerves die, the body is unable to rejuvenate them. I am barely hearing him. The finality of "you're there" is still echoing through my mind. I am ignorant about spinal cord injuries, but I am learning fast.

I soon learn the full terror of suffocation. Wanting a little more air, I start to breathe faster, and then faster still, but I can't get enough air. Soon my breaths are right on top of each other and so shallow that I am mainly moving air in my trachea. I feel I am suffocating and about to go down for the count. Therapists appear on each side of me earnestly pleading with me to breathe slower and deeper. I am in a panic now. My body is screaming at me for more air, but the therapists are urging me to breathe slower! It takes all my will to take a breath and wait a whole second before taking another. Again I take a breath and wait a long second before taking another. My efforts to take deep breaths are in vain, as my breaths remain bare whispers. My body continues to scream at me, *"Breathe faster! I need air*! *BREATHE FASTER*! *BREATHE FASTER*!" but I block it out and focus totally on the directions from my therapists. Slowly I regain control and my lungs are sustaining me again. I am totally spent physically and mentally. It is a session of struggle that will be repeated several more times in the next two weeks.

I have family and friends around me daily. The hospital allows my children, my parents and Marcia's parents to stay in vacant rooms without charge so my family can always be near me. What a blessing! I am amazed at how many friends come all the way to Provo to visit us. My family and friends provide a tremendous support group around me. They talk to me, read to me and pray with me. Just having them near is a great comfort. Their company and encouragement keep my spirits up and keep me focused on the decisions that lie before me.

My law practice must be closed down. It is like cutting off a part of me. I have spent seventeen years building and nurturing it. My clients depend on me. I must direct them to other attorneys where I know they will pay much more. In addition, I represent more than thirty children taken from their home by Child Protective Services. Many have been with me for years. Some are struggling very hard in foster care. I have been their friend and their voice in the courtroom. Now I'm just one more person who has abandoned them. These thoughts weigh on me. My secretary, Carole, works tirelessly handling all the details as I relay directions through my sister, Cindy. I have beautiful people to help me. It is easy for none of us.

How I long for Marcia. Always we have talked things through and made decisions together. Now, when there are so many changes, she is not here for me. I feel abandoned. I have a deep longing to talk with her every day. She is in a coma and only a few rooms away. Sometimes I can feel her presence with me. Dr. Gaufin says her brain injury is so serious she may not survive. If she lives, she will probably always be in an institution needing total care. It is so hard to hear, and impossible to truly believe. My conscious mind blocks it out, but somewhere below the surface I know and feel this prognosis.

I am struggling more and more with my breathing. For over a day I am nearly delirious. Some nights I am sure that if I go to sleep, I will suffocate. It makes for frightful times. My doctor understands my strong desire to stay off of a vent. He orders an unusual machine for me that looks like a large turtle shell that straps to my chest. "I am a Ninja Turtle!" I kid my children. When the machine is turned on, it sounds like a muffled vacuum cleaner. My chest expands and contracts as the machine suctions and then releases. It solves my breathing problem, but after a few days I find that I am totally dependent on this machine. If it is turned off, I become short of breath and must have it turned on within a few minutes. I am not on a vent, but I *am* tied to a large noisy machine!

Even before the accident I had considered how deeply I would miss playing the piano if my hands should ever be injured. It has happened! It has happened! To ease my pain I play various melodies as my experienced hands move up and down the keyboard in my mind. There is actual physical pain in knowing I will never again sit at a piano, take command of its keys and lose myself in its music. Many things I will never be able to do again. I am missing my piano very much.

I am surprised at how much my thoughts turn to Little League and the major league team I would have had this spring. I have always loved to manage my sons' teams. I had lots of plans for this year's team. A notebook full of detailed notes on potential players sits in my bookcase at home. Now that work is for nothing. I will never coach a team again. It's just one more thing I love that is now forever in my past.

During the day I am constantly around family or hospital personnel. If I did not have tremendous encouragement from both, I don't know how I could continue. I focus on the people around me and my spirits are generally upbeat. But at night, as I lie in my bed that rotates slowly, first to the right and then to the left, I am alone. It is quiet, with only the normal hospital background noises, but my mind is not quiet. It is moving at a feverish pitch. Unnamed feelings well up in waves from deep within me, almost overcoming me with their power. Family has always been a top priority with Marcia and me. Even before our first child was born we committed that Marcia would be a stay-at-home mom. My family eats breakfast and dinner together nearly every morning and evening. I coach most of my sons' sports teams. Marcia and I are counselors at our children's camps every summer and winter. We have invested our lives building a strong family. It has paid big dividends. Our children are doing well with their peers, with us and with God. A bowling ball has now smashed my family. Marcia and I have been taken out with one blow. My children will be subject to the whirlwinds that follow. All I have built has been taken and crushed. There are no words to express my pain. No words.

"How could this have happened?" The question reverberates in my mind. It is directed at God, but I don't formally address it to Him. My family's ministries had really come together—my law practice, Marcia and Alana in counseling kids at church, our work with the youth and many other areas. I really thought we were making a difference in the lives of people. In the blink of an eye it is all gone. In my mind I know God is in control, but I don't understand. I feel a great emptiness toward God. I have lots of time to pray, but I look the other way. I know thousands of people all across the country are praying for us and I am thankful. Still, it will be many months before I am able to seek God in my time alone.

December 22. My 22nd anniversary. I have no gift for Marcia. There is nothing to celebrate. I cannot even be with her. I am told she opens her eyes sometimes, but doesn't seem to focus on anything. I wonder if this will be our last anniversary. Tears well up in my eyes and run down my cheeks. I silently curse the hands that can't wipe away my tears. In my time alone I feel very, very alone.

December 24. A small Christmas tree with gifts sits on a table in my room. My family assures me that all of the Christmas presents Marcia and I purchased have been retrieved from Phoenix and wrapped. Marcia and I have often talked of getting our Christmas shopping done before Thanksgiving, but this is the first year we actually did it. The accident has not prevented my children from receiving nice gifts from us! At 9:00 p.m. I receive a special surprise. Six of my nurses and therapists gather around my bed to sing "We Wish You a Merry Christmas". They present me with a Heineken beer (Several days before they had asked me what I really wanted for Christmas and I jokingly replied, "A Heineken beer."). I later learn that one of them drove a considerable distance to find a Heineken because very little beer is sold in Provo and Heineken isn't available.

December 25. The hospital staff has been especially giving to me and my family from the very beginning. Today they cater a special luncheon for our families at no charge. They are amazing! I am encouraged to attend—they offer to wheel my bed into the luncheon room—but I am not feeling well enough to accept. I have had many days to see my tree from my bed. Sad thoughts have come upon me many times. But there are good thoughts too, thanks to the people around me.

Eating and drinking flat on my back is now done with ease. I have had two surgeries—spinal fusion and a pace maker insertion (when my heart stopped two different times from vagal nerve stimulation my "code reds" caused a little excitement!) and my "turtle shell" has helped my breathing. I have stabilized enough to go home to Phoenix for rehab. Marcia is slowly waking from her coma and she too is stable enough for the trip. One huge problem remains: Blue Cross refuses to pay for the med-vac transport—about $15,000. My church minister, Pastor Norm, a man of great faith, begins cold calling the handful of med-vac transport companies in the Phoenix telephone book. God has more grace for us. A company agrees to the impossible. The owner will provide a plane free of charge. The two respiratory therapists, RN and pilot who accompany us, agree to donate their time. God is bringing us home.

For me it has been a month of day-to-day survival. I have been in a hospital where the Mormon faith is very strong. I will always remember these people who have shown me such love and compassion in my time of need. Much later I learn my family has made a deep impression with the hospital staff. Seeing friends, parents and especially my children, gathered around Marcia and me, praying and caring, has struck a chord they understand. The head of the hospital is so moved by my family that we are given a 5% discount from the entire hospital bill—the ultimate compliment to my Baptist family.

David A. Treat

Five Months In St. Joseph's Hospital

My new doctor delivers a real shocker the day I arrive in Phoenix—rehab can't begin while I have the turtle shell attached to my chest. I must have a tracheostomy so I can be connected to a vent. Dr. Silverthorne, a pulmonologist, assures me that some people, over time, are able to wean themselves off the vent. "Do not lose hope," she says, trying to cheer me. But I am heartbroken. I have worked so hard to not be on a vent. I know Dr. Silverthorne is right. Sadly, I give my consent for the operation.

When I awaken from my surgery the "turtle shell" is gone. I cannot talk. A six foot hose from a vent attaches to my neck and air puffs into my lungs, giving me a breath every few seconds. I am not sure how to coordinate these artificial breaths with my own weak breaths. It is confusing and uncomfortable to my body. Tomorrow a special valve will be attached to my trach that will allow me to talk while on the vent (there have been advances since my sister was on a vent). I can't wait.

In Provo I spent over a month flat on my back. Now that the turtle shell is gone I can start to sit up in my bed. It sounds simple enough, but when my back is raised only a little I get short of breath and feel light headed. My vent is set to give me twelve breaths each minute, but I can draw extra breaths with my lungs by trying to suck in. The vent senses my effort and immediately shoots a strong, full breath of air into my lungs. I am grabbing lots of extra breaths and my back is only raised up 25 degrees. After fifteen minutes my nurse lowers me back down. She brings me up several times during the day and I struggle with my breathing and consciousness each time. I go a little higher every few days and I stay up a little longer.

Within ten days I am ready to get into a wheelchair. I must wear support hose that squeeze my legs very tightly to prevent blood from pooling in my legs. Two nurses sit me on the edge of the bed. While a third nurse holds my trach hose, the other nurses, using a slide board, move me into the chair. I am seeing stars, everything is fading out, I am losing consciousness. Quickly the chair back is lowered and my legs are brought up a little. My consciousness slowly returns, but I feel very

43

uncomfortable, almost panicky, as I grab for extra breaths that my vent can't seem to send fast enough. I want to move back into my bed, but I must stay in the chair for a very long fifteen minutes. Clearly it's going to take a while before I can sit comfortably in a chair.

Many friends come to visit me. My body is paralyzed, but my mouth works very well. The overworked information desk puts up a sign with "Treat" in large letters and printed directions on how to find my room. How good it is to have friends! My doctors are concerned my many guests are tiring me too much. I beg them not to limit my visitors. My friends are a great encouragement to me. They keep me going. With definite reservations, my doctors give in.

Marcia is always on my mind. She is only a few rooms away from me. At my urging, her bed is moved to my room. She is brought near to me and her hand reaches out for mine. She is confused that my hand does not respond to hers. I can see great distress in her eyes as, for the first time, she realizes my state of total paralysis. Although it is painful to see her distress, I am encouraged by my interaction with Marcia. Her response to me shows she has come a long way.

Activity goes on in my room even at night. Two nurses come to turn me two or three times. My lungs collect mucus, which must be suctioned out several times by running a narrow plastic tube in my trach opening and then six inches down into my lungs. Lights come on and there is loud talking at each nightly interruption. I want to plead with the nurses and respiratory therapists to talk quietly, so Marcia isn't disturbed, but I am on the night vent and I can't talk. After a few days it is clear that my care keeps Marcia awake and is impeding her recovery. Sadly I see her moved down the hall again.

In Utah, my children lived in the hospital and were in and out of my room several times each day. Now I see them for just thirty minutes when they crowd into my room two times each week. "Why do Nana and Grandpa have to be with us?" they ask. "We can take care of ourselves." They seem so brave as I talk with them from my hospital bed. I have never felt this helpless! How hard this time must be for them. When they are gone I miss them so much!

Often I wake up hoping I will discover I am back to normal and everything was just a bad dream. It doesn't happen. This is not a dream—it is reality. It seems I have had two lives—one before the accident and another afterward. I miss my old life. I miss my family, my children, my Marcia. I miss my work. I hate this hospital and this bed that I lie in all day and all night. I want my life back!

45

It is easy for me to get caught up playing the "what if" game. Last year, I unexpectedly received a large legal fee. Part of this money was used to buy our new minivan. We wouldn't have come to Utah in our former, older model van. *What if* I hadn't received this large, unexpected fee??? Kevin had planned to go out for basketball, but at the last minute decided to concentrate on weight lifting for football. If he had gone out for basketball, a scheduled game would have kept us in Phoenix for Thanksgiving. *What if* Kevin had gone out for basketball??? We made a brief stop shortly before the accident. *What if* I had taken over the driving at this stop??? The "what ifs" drive me crazy! I know there is nothing to gain by thinking about the "what ifs". I must focus on what is, and not on what might have been.

A week after I arrived at St. Joseph's Hospital, a bedsore developed on my butt. For several weeks my nurses thought it would get better, but there has been little improvement. I had hoped to be ready to go home in early March, but now it's another surgery, five weeks in recovery and starting again at square one on my rehab. As I lie on my side I am angry with my nurses who were with me the first few days I was at St. Joseph's. If they had turned me every four hours I could be in rehab and not wasting time in my bed recovering from surgery. I am learning the hard way about the care I need. My five weeks in recovery turns into two months when infection is found in the stitched area and it must be opened, cleaned and restitched. In spite of this setback, I am soon convinced St. Joseph's Hospital has the greatest nurses in the world.

While recovering from my surgery, I decide to work very hard at building enough strength in my diaphragm to support breathing without a vent. The right side of my diaphragm is paralyzed, but the left side still tries to breathe for me. My respiratory therapists give me lots of encouragement and special time. Lying flat, I am able to build to where I can breathe for two hours on my own. But if the head of the bed is raised even a little, I become short of breath and unable to sustain myself. I work very hard, but I seem to have hit a wall.

I am considering going to Craig Hospital, one of the top spinal injury hospitals in the country, for my remaining rehab. Craig would give me the opportunity to have top quality spinal injury physicians and rehab specialists in an environment with many other quadriplegics. However, it would also mean going to Colorado Springs for care. It would be very difficult to be separated from family and friends for several months, but I begin mentally preparing myself for going away. Arrangements are made for Craig doctors to visit me at St. Joseph's for an evaluation. After enduring a battery of tests, I anxiously await the written report. I am hoping the Craig doctors are optimistic about getting me off the vent and possibly even about restoring some movement to my limbs. The report finally comes, but I am tremendously disappointed. My cord injury is so high that the Craig doctors anticipate I will only be able to breathe free of the vent if I lie quietly, flat in bed. If I want to lead an active life, I will always need the vent. This report hits me hard. Now my vent dependency seems more permanent than ever.

One thing gives me great comfort. I have been the husband and father God intended me to be. My wife and children have always had my attention and my time. They know I love them deeply because I have been involved in every aspect of their lives. Counseling a camp or managing a sports team may now be impossible. Even helping with my child's homework will be difficult. I have done these things and much, much more. I have no regrets.

Marcia's progress is greater than her Provo doctors thought possible. Praise God! She is surprising her doctors with her abilities. She is taking her first steps, with assistance, and talking better and with a greater vocabulary almost every day. We all felt certain she had more inside of her than she was given credit for in Provo. Now she is proving it!

I am told that it is possible for me to drive an electric wheelchair even though I am unable to move my fingers or arms. The sip and puff chair has a hard plastic straw positioned near my mouth. This straw connects to a flexible cable that goes to the controls located on the back of the chair. The chair is controlled by blowing air into the straw or sipping air back from the straw. A puff into the straw sends the chair forward. A sip from the straw either stops the chair or, if the chair isn't moving, it backs the chair up. A gentle puff turns the chair to the right, and a gentle sip turns the chair to the left. Simple enough, right? *Right.*

I practice in a large, open room where two cafeteria-style chairs are set up twenty feet apart. First I circle the chairs clockwise and then counterclockwise. After I can do circles I begin doing figure eights around the chairs—first to the right and then to the left. A visitor says it is amusing to watch me practice as I hit a chair or bang a wall with my wheelchair from time to time. It takes a while to learn the breath technique for driving this "vehicle". As I master figure eights, the chairs are moved closer together requiring smaller figure eights. Soon I'm ready for an obstacle course. My physical therapist enjoys setting up challenging driving assignments for me.

I practice driving my chair twenty to thirty minutes most days. Before long I am ready for an excursion outside. The amazing technology of this chair is giving me greatly desired independence.

Susie, my physical therapist, decides to have me practice with my chair in the parking lot. As I weave around among the cars the battery on my vent signals it is low. We head back toward the hospital right away, but the battery unexpectedly goes totally dead. I'm unable to talk without the vent. There is no danger, because I can breathe on my own for two or three minutes and an electrical outlet is available directly inside the hospital. But my physical therapist panics. She is afraid I am suffocating and takes off running with my heavy chair toward the hospital entrance. We are approaching the narrow gate in a chain link fence that borders the parking lot at an incredible speed. I am scared to death. We crash through the gate and continue toward the private entrance to the hospital at break neck speed. Susie screams for someone to open the door. My chair scrapes the doorway as we pass through and I'm now headed for a wall, full speed ahead. SLAM! My wheelchair is finally at rest. Susie fumbles with my vent cord trying to plug it in. With power restored, a full breath of air flows into my lungs. Susie tries to catch her breath as she pants loudly at my side. "Susie," I say smiling, "I was doing fine until you tried to kill me with your crazy driving!" She is the subject of much kidding in the weeks that follow.

Little League's opening day is in early April. My doctors agree to grant me a day-pass from the hospital so that I can attend. I am excited! Donna, one of my nurses, graciously volunteers to go with me, since this is my first excursion away from the hospital. At the field, team pictures are being taken, carnival games are being played and the first Little League games are underway. Everyone is here. I see many coaches and parents who have been my friends. They all act glad to see me, but I sense they are also stunned by my appearance. The many kids I see who once played for me give me an awkward, "Hi Coach," before making a hasty getaway. A hose coming out of my neck attaches to a small vent that audibly pumps air into my lungs. My speech is in measured sentences that have occasional breaks while I await the next breath of air. It all makes quite an impact the first time friends see me. I do not feel well physically. It is a long and very tough day for me. But emotionally, it is a great day, because I feel the sun on my face and I'm thinking and talking baseball!

I have continued to work on weaning myself off the vent, but can manage only five to ten minutes on my own when I am sitting up in bed. My breaths remain extremely shallow. One morning, while I am sitting up in bed, my nurse leans me forward. Upon leaning me back, the vent hose accidentally comes loose, but she doesn't notice. Disconnected from the vent I can make no sound. An alarm is supposed to sound, but it fails. My nurse leaves the room unaware of my desperate situation. People walk by my room and I try to get their attention by mouthing, "Help me!" But I am ignored! Breathing hard, but very shallow, I realize I am losing ground. As the minutes go by, I am struggling harder and harder for air, and it is difficult to remain calm. I wonder if this is my day to die. My nurse comes in my room. She sees my desperate eyes and my hurried, weak gasps for air and in horror discovers the loose hose. The hose is reattached and delicious air flows deeply into my lungs again. I make it today, but what about tomorrow? Suffocation haunts me.

I wake up in the morning with extreme pressure in my chest. It is like an elephant is sitting on it. The weight is so heavy that I don't think the vent can expand my lungs. It can, of course. The huge "weight" is just an illusion—a very painful illusion. My whole day is spent lying in bed, but it doesn't get any better. This is my first bad day with my severely spastic chest. I will have one or two very bad days each week for the rest of my hospital stay. If my Baclofen dose is increased, it seems to help, but I am limited on how much Baclofen I can take orally. It is decided that I will benefit from an internal Baclofen pump. It's back to the operating room—*again*!

It has been many months since I have been to church. I am missing worship and fellowship with the church family very much. I am spending some time with God, but I still feel distant from Him. James, Chapter 1, says I should count it joy when I have trials. I know God is with me, but hospitals are very lonely places, and my life seems very hard. The future that looms ahead scares me. It is difficult to feel the joy of the Lord in my life.

Night is my worst time. That's when the questions come—questions that torment me. When I leave the hospital I will need twenty-four hour care. I don't have nearly enough money to pay for such care for very long. I wonder if I will lose my house. Will I have to go into an institution for care at the government's expense? Who will care for my children? What will become of Marcia? How did everything get so messed up?!!! Emotional pain wells up within me, and involuntarily I cry out. My nurse comes. She knows I am hurting, and asks if I want to talk. How can she understand? She doesn't know me or my family—not really. I am not ready to let everything out.

One of my respiratory therapists comes to me for advice on a child support problem. I talk with him about what to expect, but advise he will need a lawyer. He says his brother knows a good family law attorney that he will contact. The next night he comes to me and says, "My brother said, 'Call David Treat. He's really good.'" It's a small world!

My attorney friend, Bud Roberts, has good news. He has talked with a lawyer in a firm that handles product liability cases and is informed I may have a car design case against Chrysler. I feel like I'm grasping at straws, but I agree to retain the firm. In addition, I had a million dollar umbrella policy that would have covered this accident. Unfortunately, I put off paying the premium a few weeks before the accident and the company claims the policy has now gone out of force. Bud researches this claim carefully and concludes the insurance company has a strong defense. Nevertheless, he marshals a good argument in my favor. I'm hoping one of these claims will come through for me.

I have been attending a weekly support group of the rehab patients. All have significant paralysis. Many are in wheel chairs. We talk about our problems and our feelings. Most of the patients are depressed. Their injuries are bad, but their life situations make things much worse. Very few have supportive people around them. Some have spouses leaving them. None have injuries nearly as severe as mine. I would switch places with none of them.

I am very thankful for all of the special people who step forward to meet my family's needs. Marcia's parents drop everything in North Carolina to be with my children and manage my household. People in our church bring them prepared meals five times each week. David Kimmerle, who owns a car dealership, gives them use of a new car for the five months they are in Phoenix. Frank Rigo gives his frequent flyer miles for airline tickets. Alana moves back home to help with her brothers. My parents visit me every evening—they never miss. Pastor Norm visits me and Marcia three or four times each week. He takes care of many things that make my life so much easier. He even has a van built to meet my needs. A friend who has a car painting business gratuitously custom paints my van. Carole Gatlin agrees to act as our conservator so our many bills, especially medical bills, can be paid. Attorney Kathleen Kassmann has Carole appointed by the court, and attorney Bud Roberts battles with our insurance carrier, all at no charge. Church friends make significant changes to my home to make it comfortable for my care needs when I go home. Through our family and friends, in Phoenix and across the country thousands, or perhaps tens of thousands, of people pray for us. God and His people are carrying us.

Bad things sometimes happen to God's people. He doesn't promise otherwise. He simply promises to be with them every step of the way. I knew this before the accident. It has been difficult to accept in my own life. But God has been with my family since the first moments after the accident and He has carried me. My time alone with God is a strong time for me again.

It is time to prepare for going home. I very much want to leave, but I have fears about my ability to survive on the outside. For six months I have been in hospitals. RNs, respiratory therapists and physical therapists have managed my care. Now I must get by with a Certified Nursing Assistant (CNA). My care is very demanding, both day and night. Mistakes can have severe, possibly fatal, consequences for me. It is frightening to leave the security the hospital has provided.

I have no idea how to find a CNA to provide the care I need. Financial reasons dictate that I hire a live-in. One of my nurses knows a CNA interested in the position. My nurses will train him. The trainee struggles very hard at moving me into my chair, a job always needing two nurses in the hospital. On the third day of training he doesn't show up. I can't reach him. I never see him again. This is my first experience in hiring help.

I am told I will be transferred to an outside facility unless I have a CNA trained and ready to care for me within one week. The thought of transferring somewhere else is very hard for me. I feel like my friends at St. Joseph's are abandoning me to strangers when I need them desperately for help in finding and training a worker. An ad is run in the paper and I hire a new attendant two days later. He trains over the next several days and I'm finally ready to go home. I have had a roller coaster of emotions this week. Now I must adjust to a stranger handling my care. The hospital is pushing me out of the nest and I am terrified I can't fly on my own. I remind myself I am in God's care. I'm glad God is in charge because my newly hired worker is about to say goodbye!

May 1994—Life On The Outside

I sit in my wheelchair, strapped in my new van, speeding toward home. The sound of the vent as it pushes air into my lungs every few seconds mixes with the hum of the van engine and the noises of the road. Anxious thoughts race through my mind. I have said I want to be home, but now the prospect scares me. I have already had two overnight home visits, with Kevin and Alana providing my care, but this is very different—now I'm on my own for good. My bed at the hospital no longer awaits in case of problems. Mike, my 60-year-old, newly trained attendant, will provide my care day and night. I barely know Mike. Now he will live in my home.

Derrick, a respiratory therapist from Western Medical, meets us as we arrive home. He gives Mike a short training session on the vent, making sure he understands the different alarms and how the hoses are connected and cleaned.

Derrick goes over the supplies he is delivering and shows Mike how to order more supplies when needed. We are given a telephone number we can call day or night if we have a vent problem. Derrick will check back with us in a week to make sure everything is going all right. Western Medical and Derrick have given me a much-needed shot of confidence.

Marcia came home from the hospital a month ago. She sleeps in the master bedroom where we have slept together for 14 years. I have a hospital bed with an air mattress in an adjoining bedroom, which was previously Alana's room. It has been modified by church friends to be larger and to have a large adjoining bathroom to accommodate my needs. Our large playroom is now a small office—the sacrifice to create the modifications to my room. Mike will sleep on a daybed in the corner of my room. So many changes.

I am apprehensive about my first night, but it goes quite well. Mike does a great job. At the alarm clock's ring, he turns me. When I signal that I need his help, by activating a chime with my head, he wakes up quickly and comes to me. In the morning, after breakfast, he gets me into my chair. It is summer, so my children are not in school. I spend quality time with them I have missed for a long time. In the evening we have dinner around the table. We are truly together as a family again. Things are going well!

An ad is run in the paper for an attendant to work every other weekend so that Mike will have a break from my care. Mike makes an announcement I dread hearing. He has decided to accept a position with someone else. However, one of the people who responded to the ad is interested in the live-in position. Mike agrees to stay on long enough to train him. Mike has been with me only a week. Now he's gone and 19-year-old Alex has replaced him. I had been warned by my nurses to expect caregiver turnover. I hadn't expected it this soon.

Marcia has made tremendous strides. She is amazing! She is more than amazing—she is a true miracle. She is able to walk with a walker; she talks with a slight speech impediment, but with a pretty normal vocabulary. She looks after her own personal needs. A stranger meeting her would think she seemed normal. But Marcia struggles in a number of areas that she works on daily at the Arizona Day Hospital. She is truly a walking testament to the power of the prayers that have blanketed us. Her doctors say she will continue making progress for years.

Many times I would like to give Marcia encouragement and comfort with a hug or just a simple touch. It is very hard to see her, but be unable to touch her. She says I should try to express my touches with words of love. I try, but it's impossible. My arms ache to reach out and gather her to me. Words without touches are empty.

Jeffrey has started talking back to Marcia. Because of her brain injury, she has difficulty processing his words quickly and giving an appropriate response. The dispute frequently elevates into a verbal fight. I hear most of these fights from my room. Even when I am present I can rarely get control of the situation because I can't elevate my voice enough to be heard. Everyone is very upset afterwards. I can't believe what is happening. Before the accident Jeffrey always respected his mother. I feel very helpless. Marcia is vulnerable and Jeffrey is angry inside. Before the accident he had two parents totally involved in his life. Jeffrey knows the life he would have had, but which has now slipped away forever. In my heart I am crying. I have lost hold of the leadership reins in my family and I'm not sure how to pick them up. I take this matter to God.

I am able to go to church again! It has been so long in coming. It feels good to worship in God's house with my family and other believers, but I am very self-conscious about the way I look. The hose coming out of my neck and the vent on the back of my chair, puffing away, especially make me feel that I look weird. Everyone smiles as they greet me, but I see their aghast looks as they stare from a distance at the man who once was David Treat.

I am getting a strong dose of humility. Before the accident I walked tall with confidence and poise. I helped many people in need. I received many pats on the back. I was a giver. Now I am a taker. It is a mental challenge to reverse my roles. The truth is, I can't do a single thing, not even breathe, without help. "Could you please scratch my left eyebrow, move that chair over, give me a bite of salad?" I am always asking. I get no pats on the back. Female friends instinctively kiss me on the forehead as they would a small, hurt child. Once I commanded respect, now I see looks of sadness and sympathy.

A panoply of medical equipment goes with me whenever I leave my home. I need a mobile suction kit, with a generous supply of suction catheters, so mucus can be suctioned from my lungs as needed. In addition, I carry equipment to manually pump air into my lungs should my vent fail. Finally, there is a supply of canulas, various connectors, a thermometer and my reading glasses.

Jeffrey's Little League team is struggling. This is the team that I would have managed. My former assistant coach, George, is the manager.

George invites me to a practice to work with the pitchers. Unfortunately, the field is fenced, the only gate is locked and I can't get inside. Barriers! I have a pitcher set up next to the fence to work with him as I give instructions from my side of the fence. I work with four different pitchers and see great potential, but they need lots of work. Being a coach again gives me a high, but it is extremely draining physically. George wants me to continue working with the pitchers. How I would like to do this, but it is getting hotter and I can't tolerate May afternoons. One of the subtle consequences of a high cervical injury is the inability to sweat. Heat and direct sun are my enemies. I am not able to come to another practice.

In studying my bank statement I am surprised to see two ATM withdrawals of fifty dollars each. Marcia and I don't use the ATM. We decide it must be a mistake. I tell Marcia that if the bank insists the statement is correct, I will request a picture of the person who made the withdrawals. Alex seems surprised a picture record exists for every ATM transaction. A few days later he confesses to using the card. Now I have a difficult decision. It should be easy. I should tell Alex to clear out that very day. But my life depends on having a caregiver. I have many demanding care needs that could be life threatening. Alex has been working out fairly well. Finding and training another live-in caregiver may not be easy. I decide to give Alex another chance.

Kevin is practicing for football and I look forward to the first game in mid-September. Last season I was the proud father with a video camera at every home and away game, creating a record of my freshman son, a starting running back for the varsity team. His small high school lacks a lighted field and so games are played on Saturday mornings. This year I will only be able to watch the first half of the games in September and early October because these are hot months in Phoenix.

A small black pressure sore has appeared on my butt. Alex says there was no warning. At my bath there was no sign of a problem. Two days later, at my next bath, it was there. He admits he has no experience with pressure sores, but hopes he can get this one healed. I've heard this line before and have grave concern I am headed for another surgery. Time in my chair is significantly reduced to help the healing process. A small hard black area on the outside of each foot near my baby toe appears. Who would have thought my well-worn tennis shoes would be too tight for my paralyzed feet?

Eddie will be getting married October 1st in Kingman, Arizona. We all are planning to go to Laughlin to stay overnight at Harrah's Casino where Eddie and his fiancée are employed. The following morning we'll travel the short distance north to Kingman for the wedding. It will be my first overnight away from home and I am a little anxious, but nothing will keep me from my son's wedding! We are all excited as plans for the wedding trip are made.

My lungs are feeling congested. Each day they are worse. One evening my breathing is so labored I'm not sure I can make it through the night. My lungs are burning and I can't get enough oxygen. An ambulance is called and I'm on my way to St. Joseph's Hospital ER. I soon learn that I have an advanced case of pneumonia. I've been away from St. Joseph's for four months. Now I'm back with a pressure sore on my butt and burning lungs that require oxygen enriched air. What really makes me sad is that I will not be able to be present at my son's fast approaching wedding. Life is hard.

There has been concern for some time that Alex isn't keeping my room and bathroom clean enough. Cleanliness is especially important, because my trach opening provides direct entrance into my lungs and makes me exceptionally susceptible to respiratory infections. Another serious problem arises with Alex. When my room and closet are thoroughly cleaned while I'm in the hospital, several pornographic magazines are discovered. Another magazine is found under the living room couch. Alex must go.

October 1st is a very long day. Eddie is my oldest child (age 22) and the first to get married. My struggle with pneumonia has been very hard. Three different IV antibiotics were pumped into me, while I struggled with my breathing for two weeks on oxygen-enriched air. Tomorrow I have surgery on my pressure sores (one on my butt and one on each foot). I'm not sure how much more my body can take. I am lonely and discouraged. Will I live to be at any of my children's weddings? It is impossible for me to avoid this question.

I must hire a new caregiver before I can be discharged from the hospital. The job is too difficult for one person to handle with every other weekend off. I decide to hire two caregivers. Each will work three and one-half days of the week. An ad is run and interviews are scheduled in my hospital room. Unfortunately, most interviews are no-shows and of the few people who come, only one, Tony, is interested in the position. Informed of my problem, Tony agrees to work both shifts until I can hire another worker. I'm going home!

Pastor Norm knows our caregiver expense is eating up our financial resources. He is a constant source of ideas. With our permission, he writes to about fifty of our friends, explaining our situation and asking if they will commit to contributing fifteen dollars each month toward our caregiver expense. We pay out over three thousand dollars each month for caregivers, but the money contributed each month by my friends, in response to this letter, makes a real difference.

Kevin comes to me. "What's wrong, Dad? All I do anymore is schoolwork and football. Football just isn't fun anymore." Last year all Kevin did during football season was schoolwork and football and he had the time of his life. When I probe a little deeper I find the real problem. Last year there were seven seniors who provided strong leadership for the football team. This year there are only seven or eight junior and senior starters and none are leaders. Coach has asked Kevin to assume leadership of the team. Last year Kevin had several seniors encouraging him and telling him what to do. This year the team leadership is squarely on his shoulders. The upperclassmen don't like taking instruction from a sophomore. That's why "football just isn't fun anymore". I'm not involved in Kevin's life like I once was, but when I have conversations with him like this, I still feel like a Dad.

Tony has been working out well in that he is very competent at my care. Time is Tony's glaring weakness. He makes us late for everything. In addition, when Tony leaves for a short errand he sometimes doesn't return for hours. This becomes a greater problem as Tony's time with us grows.

It's a nice evening after dinner and I decide to go outside with Tony. I follow the sidewalk around to the side of my house and notice a small hedge needs watering. While Tony goes for the hose, I begin to turn my chair around. Accidentally, I back up too far allowing one wheel of my chair to slip onto the curb. My chair rocks sharply as one set of wheels roles backward into the street. I tumble onto the asphalt headfirst. When Tony comes back with the hose moments later he sees my crumpled body on the ground. He is terrified I might be badly hurt. Fortunately, I only have a nasty cut and large lump above my left eyebrow. It's a helpless feeling to fall without being able to stick out an arm or twist my body. I lead with my head whether I like it or not. It's a good thing I've got a hard head!

Bud Roberts has kept me updated on his research and his conversations with the insurance company regarding my umbrella policy. Up until now, the insurance company has given him little hope they would negotiate a settlement. Today he has good news. The company has indicated they will make an offer. "Might they offer as much as three hundred thousand dollars?" I ask. "I really have no idea," Bud responds. "I'll call you later this week." Two weeks later I have a check in my hand for six hundred thousand dollars. WOW!!! Bud and God really worked on the people at the insurance company! I won't need caregiver funds from my friends anymore.

My internal Baclofen pump delivers medicine directly on my spinal cord. Since the pump was implanted in June, I have had to regularly increase the Baclofen dose to control my painful spastic chest wall. My dose is now extremely high and cannot be increased further. I am not feeling well, my weight is down, and the smallest setback may be my last. To me it seems unlikely I will live much longer. As I consider these "facts", my heart goes out to my wife and children. I won't be there for so many difficult things to come. More than anything else, I want them to know how much they were loved and how much joy they brought to me. Two-paged, single-spaced letters are composed in my mind for Marcia and for each of my four children. Mom Begley writes the words down as I dictate to her. Each letter is an emotional and physical struggle, but once finished, my mind is at ease.

My 22nd anniversary was spent in the hospital in Provo, just a few weeks after the accident. Emotionally, it was the hardest day of my life and one of the few days I allowed myself to be depressed. What a difference a year makes.

My 23rd anniversary is spent in my own home. Life is still hard, as Marcia is struggling in many areas and my physical health is on the edge. But Marcia's condition and prognosis are totally changed. She has been restored to us. Our financial condition is strong. We are together as a family. There is much to celebrate. Leslie Reeves and the senior high youth group give us a special gift. They deliver a terrific anniversary dinner. A year ago last fall we had a leadership role with these kids. Now they are bringing joy to our special night.

Continuing a longstanding Christmas Eve tradition, my family, together with my sister Cindy's family (who is here for the holidays), have lasagna dinner at Mom and Dad's. We then attend Christmas Eve service together before gathering in my home to read the story of Jesus' birth from Luke, sing some carols and share our many memories of Christmases past. We also open a few presents. When everyone is gone, Kevin and Alana pack the stockings and lay them in front of the fireplace. Kevin is my caregiver tonight. Previous years the kids would have gotten Marcia and me up on Christmas morning at 7:00 sharp, but this year everyone sleeps in an extra hour. After opening all the presents, we get ready to go out for breakfast—another longstanding tradition. My family is still a family!

1995

With more money available, I am now able to hire Jennie to work a night shift. She begins the first week of January. Two weeks later I hire Gabriel to work every weekend. Finally I don't have a live-in worker, but instead, a team of workers. My payroll has increased substantially, but it is worth every penny.

Alana asks permission to move out of our home. She feels it's time for her to separate from her core family and move in with school friends. We depend on Alana tremendously. As a licensed driver she is transportation for shopping, running errands and rides for Jeffrey. More than this, she is emotional glue in our family and she is female company for Marcia. As Marcia and I talk about Alana's request, we realize how much we rely on her. The thought of her leaving strikes feelings of panic inside of us. But she is right. For her good, she needs to be on her own. With great reluctance, we give our permission.

My chest pain continues to be a serious problem. I have adjusted to my paralysis quite well, but I feel my chest is destroying me. I dread mornings because it is such a painful struggle to be in the sitting position in my bed. Many mornings I sit up for sixty seconds and then must quickly lie down because I'm struggling to breathe and the pressure on my chest is great. I can breathe easier lying flat in bed, but I won't let my chest defeat me. I sit up again for two difficult minutes and then lie down. After fighting for an hour, I am finally able to sit up, but my chest still hurts. Sometimes it feels like an elephant is sitting on my chest. Other times it feels like I am in a suffocatingly tight straight jacket that is tightened a notch with every breath. It seems strange to see my arms lying loosely at my sides, but to feel them wrapped in a tight, painful squeeze around my body.

My doctor refers me to a neurologist who is a pain specialist. She wants me to take morphine. After a long discussion, I agree to try this addictive drug. My first few doses seem to make a little difference, but I'm not sure if it is helping because some days I feel better than others. The morphine I take is an innocuous looking green liquid, but it is a powerful substance. After taking it for two weeks I begin to have anxiety attacks. For short periods of time I'm convinced I'm going to die and my family is falling apart. With panic in my voice, I give a strong measure of these feelings to anyone unlucky enough to be in my room or call on the telephone. In my saner moments I wonder if I am going crazy. In addition, I begin to feel my body hunger for my next dose. I am becoming addicted. Morphine is reducing my chest pain very little, if at all. Clearly, it is not a solution. My doctor begins having me experiment with combinations of other medications. These help with my breathing, but not with the huge pressure and pain in my chest.

Marcia and I have been going to Kevin's sports events. I have managed to see three football games, most of his home basketball games and now I'm watching his baseball games. We haven't been to any of his track meets yet. Church and Kevin's sports competitions get me out of the house. Few other things do.

I have stopped trying to understand why the accident happened. I only know God has not forgotten me. He has taken care of my every need. Time with God in prayer and praise is a priority in my life. Before the accident my life was fast paced. Finding blocks of time for prayer and meditation was difficult. Now I have time—lots of time. Many nights I lie awake for hours at a time. This becomes my special time with God. I mentally talk things through with God. I have many requests to bring to Him about my wife and children. Many things I cannot do for them, but I *can* pray. I also spend time listening—really listening to God. God is working on me.

"I'm my beloved's and she is mine…" These beautiful words from "Song of Solomon" describe the relationship I had with Marcia before the accident. I knew with absolute certainty this relationship would never change. It was a given in my life. But it's not that way now. I had never considered the consequences of a brain injury. To me, it seems Marcia's brain injury erased her feelings for me. There are additional reasons for distant feelings between us. She was totally abandoned by me for the five and one-half months of my hospitalization. Since getting home I am still unable to meet her needs. She needs help in doing things—getting around, fixing occasional meals, cleaning up and so many others. I can't help her. She needs help in dealing with Jeffrey, but I'm in my room and not feeling well so much of the time that I can't assist. She needs love and comfort, but I offer only empty words. My beloved needs so much, and I can offer virtually nothing. This is the part of being paralyzed I hate!

Marcia is correct when she says I don't understand her. She won't trust me with her feelings. The few feelings she does share make it clear her interpretation of my words and actions is totally different than my actual thoughts and intentions. I can't convince her of this. We don't seem to be able to make a connection. There is a huge emptiness inside of me. My best friend is no more. The love I have fed on for 25 years evaporated in the few moments after the accident. My ability to win Marcia again has been severely compromised. If I could do things to help her, or touch her in love and comfort, I could back up my words with actions. I have *nothing* to offer Marcia but my words, and my words are so, so inadequate. I feel lost from her.

Occasionally, I still work on breathing off of the vent. Today I have a breakthrough. I breathe comfortably sitting in my chair, disconnected from the vent, for thirty minutes. Amazing! Up until today, five to ten minutes in the sitting position was my "gasping" limit. The following day I am able to be off the vent for one full hour. I feel like I'm on my way. By the end of the week, I can do four hours on my own in my chair. Sunday I go to church praising God with the vent in my van (a precautionary measure). Within another week I am off the vent all day. Each breath requires effort, but my diaphragm is now strong enough to keep going all day long.

Suffocation no longer haunts me. A large weight has been lifted from me.

A month later my neurosurgeon telephones and I mention to him that I am no longer on the vent during the day. "What did you just say?" he asks incredulously. I repeat that I'm no longer using the vent during the day. "I thought I heard you say that," he says excitedly. "I'm glad I talked to you today, David. You have reminded me that miracles still happen."

Tony is an hour or more late to work every day. He always seems tired, sometimes even going to sleep at work. I strongly suspect he is using drugs. I need to fire him, but I've got a problem. Jennie doesn't know most of my care needs and isn't available during the day. Gabriel works fulltime during the week at another job. If I fire Tony, I have no one. He knows this and takes advantage of me because of it. I have an intolerable situation, but I don't have an answer, so I limp along with Tony.

Friends of ours tell us about Chad, a CNA who might be interested in working for me. I set up an interview with Chad for Sunday afternoon. On Friday, Tony has a car problem and doesn't even come to work. All day I lie in bed praying I will not need to be suctioned, because no caregiver is with me until Kevin gets home from school. Friday night I telephone Tony and let him go.

Now I am desperate for a daytime caregiver. Beginning Monday I have no one. I take this to God. I tell Him the huge size of my problem. I leave it in His hands. On Sunday my interview with Chad goes very well. He is interested in being on my team of workers and will start tomorrow. Tony has been a cancer on my household. Chad is a twenty-year-old, energetic breath of fresh air. He is also an answer to prayer.

Dr. Pam Klonoff, the psychologist who counsels with Marcia at Arizona Day Hospital, wants to counsel with me also. She wants to get more input on Marcia's family situation and to help me know how to understand Marcia better. I am hesitant because I feel poorly so often. I am afraid it will be too much for me to travel weekly to Pam's office. Pam understands and volunteers to drive the lengthy distance to my home for the counseling. Incredible! Pam is great! She not only helps me understand Marcia's difficulties, but is also a good listener. There are many things I haven't felt free to discuss with anyone. Just getting them out is therapeutic.

September 1st is Marcia's birthday. Many painful feelings weigh on my heart as I remember past birthdays and the happiness we shared. My thoughts begin to take shape and a poem I call, "For Marcia", emerges. It is emotionally draining to dictate the lines to my caregiver. It's the first poem I've ever written. My gift to her has come forth from my pain.

I have been off the vent during the day for several months. I would like very much to be off it at night as well. Each breath still requires significant effort. It seems impossible to sleep when my diaphragm is working so hard. In November I decide to stay off of the vent all night. The first night the effort of breathing keeps me from sleep. However, the next night I go to sleep off the vent and I sleep most of the night. I'm there—totally free of the vent! The feeling is incredible!

1996

My voice is very gradually getting weaker, but I don't notice it for a long time. Eventually, I realize I can't be heard in groups where background noise is present. I can't elevate the volume of my voice above that needed to be heard in a quiet room. At night I sometimes wake up with a headache. One night my headache is so severe I decide to go to the emergency room. While there, my headache subsides. I am released after they do tests which show I have an elevated level of carbon dioxide in my blood. Dr. Silverthorne calls me later in the day and says I'm not breathing deeply enough at night to flush the carbon dioxide from my blood. I must go back onto the vent at night. I am very disappointed at this news. I have enjoyed being totally free of the vent very much. Following Dr. Silverthorne's directions, I spend the next night on the vent. In the morning I awaken with a strong enough voice to be heard in crowds—an incredible improvement in just one night. My diaphragm is strong enough to support me during the day, but it needs a rest at night. I now know its limits.

Touches—physical connections—mean so much to us humans. A handshake on greeting a new acquaintance, a light hug between friends and a firm embrace between lovers, are just a few examples of important touches. We use touch in our society a great deal to convey feeling and caring. I know. I have watched touches given and received from the outside. I can give no touches. I especially need to give touches when interacting with family members. In times of hurting, I need desperately to be able to simply extend my hand to lightly touch my child's arm, or to squeeze my wife to me and hold her a few moments before softly assuring her, "It's going to be ok. I love you so much." As I interact with my family, I am more and more aware how important touches are for showing compassion, expressing love and in making my words sound genuine. Words without touches are sterile. I have not found a way to break through this one. My greatest handicap is my inability to give touches.

I have almost given up hope in getting any relief from my chest pain. My neurologist is out of ideas and doesn't even return my telephone calls. I understand why Dr. Kevorkian's services are in demand. Some days I just want to have my coffin nailed shut. Many times my pain is nearly unbearable. It has continued to increase and I do not want to contemplate my future. This is another issue I bring before God daily. Pam suggests a second opinion and recommends a neurologist. This doctor arranges for me to have a one-time consultation with a neurologist at the Mayo Clinic (we have a local branch in the Phoenix area). For the first time I hear a doctor say he has a few patients, with high cervical injuries, who have symptoms similar to mine. "I get the hard cases," Dr. Gonzales explains. "You will probably always have some chest pain, but the combination of medications I prescribe should make a significant difference in your symptoms." I am relieved to hear a doctor talk with experience and confidence about helping me. I thought my case was unique. The medications he recommends do, in fact, help me greatly. I still have difficult days, but most are good. I feel my life has been given back to me!

Some would say, simply, that modern medicine has finally come through for me. I see things quite differently. I have been petitioning God with my health for months. God has directed me to perhaps the only doctor in the Phoenix area who knows how to treat my symptoms. God has delivered me.

Many mornings I awaken early. As I lie in bed, I think about Marcia. She says the good times are all behind her. She rarely smiles and seems to not have the ability to laugh. There is no joy in her life. Each day is simply to be endured, and even this is done with difficulty. She and Jeffrey continue to be at odds, which breaks my heart. She says he hates her. Many times when Priscilla, my nighttime caregiver, gets me up in the morning, my eyes are teary from my thoughts. My paralysis seems as nothing compared to what has happened to Marcia. My heart cries for her.

Alana comes to me for advice. She has been dating Allen for several years. Listening to the vows exchanged at weddings, she is not sure she is ready to make such vows to Allen. She is not absolutely sure he is "the one". It is a very difficult decision to break up with Allen. I tell her to date other guys and not go back to Allen unless she knows she can't live without him. I am surprised that in only three weeks she is back seeing Allen. "Now I *know*, Daddy," she says to me with sparkles in her eyes, "I can't be away from him!" Two weeks later Allen telephones to ask if it would be all right for him to come by to talk with Marcia and me. We soon learn he wants permission to marry our daughter. In May of next year I will have a son-in-law. Wow!

Jeffrey is thirteen and has been lobbying hard to single date. When he is met by our stonewall refusal, he announces, "In six months I'll be fourteen and then I can single date." He is confounded to learn no single dates at fourteen either. Jeffrey is definitely interested in girls and has been requesting a covenant ring. Marcia and I agree it is time, so we visit a jeweler with Jeffrey to have his ring designed. When it is ready, I take Jeffrey (Marcia got to take our daughter, I get to take our sons) out to a nice restaurant of his choice for the covenant ceremony. During dinner, any question regarding females and sex is open for discussion. After dinner, the covenant ceremony begins. There are three covenants Jeffrey will make before God and me: 1) that he will not have sexual intercourse or engage in inappropriate touching with a girl, until he is married, 2) that he will not take the ring off until his wedding night, when he will give it to his bride, 3) that when anyone remarks about his ring, he will tell them of its meaning. It is a solemn ceremony, conducted similar to the vows exchanged at a wedding and ending in prayer. I sure love being a Dad!

Before my paralysis, my yard had gardens brimming with flowers nearly all year long. Now my yard has none. While at Home Depot, Chad and I see pots filled with spring flowers. I buy seven of them to brighten up the front yard. We also buy some flower six-packs which Chad plants in four large empty pots I already have around the swimming pool. Flowers have always brightened my spirits!

I am getting out of the home more. It is much easier to go out because I leave the vent at home. I don't think I look weird anymore since the vent hose no longer attaches to my neck. I get plenty of looks as I cruise the malls, because people are curious about how I am directing my chair. Sometimes strangers are even bold enough to ask about this. I tell them I just focus my mind on where I want to go and the chair does the rest. "Oh...h...h," is a common response. People will believe anything! I regularly see mothers grab their small children from my pathway. I don't blame them. Driving by blowing air through a straw is too amazing to be trusted!

Pam has been counseling with me for over a year. We agree that regular counseling is no longer needed. If Marcia or I feel a need, she is always available. I know Pam and the other workers at Arizona Day Hospital have made a crucial difference for Marcia. I will always remember Pam's dedication to us, which included traveling to our home so I could be a part of the counseling process.

In October, Kim, Alana's best friend, is going to China as a missionary for two years. Alana has known Kim since she was two years old. Kim has spent so many weekends in our home over the years that I sometimes think of her as my second daughter. I commit that I will pray for Kim daily and write to her regularly, so she knows friends in Phoenix remember her, in thought and prayer. In my work as an attorney I am required to be a good persuasive writer, but I have never written creatively for fun. In my letters to Kim I write humorously with stories, including some past memories of her, in an effort to entertain her.

A number of years ago, I learned one of Kim's "claims to fame" when I pulled my chair up to her table at a restaurant. There sat sweet, lovely, thirteen-year-old Kimberly, competing with a group of boys in a belching contest!—AND WINNING!!! Remembering this, I challenge Kim to a belching contest. I suggest that we commit our belches to tape, so that an impartial panel can judge them. "Have you ever considered that a well crafted belch is choreographed similar to a ballet?" I ask. "Can't you just hear a belch modeled from the following dance moves: the dancer begins with a graceful spin balancing on one toe, poises there for a moment, dives gracefully toward the floor where she then recovers and makes fleeting jumps that go higher and higher, finally ending in a death throw (hopefully at center stage)? As with any art form, variations are endless. Imagine 'Swan Lake' performed by an accomplished belcher! Doesn't the thought give you goose bumps?!!" I have lots of fun with the belching theme. In other letters I tell legendary tales about The Honorable Office Rocker. My imaginary judge is good for many laughs as he proudly announces that his young son, who he calls "Blame", actually is Office Blame Rocker VII. My letters are therapeutic. They challenge my mind to move beyond its boring existence in its bed-bound body. More than this, I have found a way to be a giver. I get some pats on the back. They feel incredibly good!

My children's school has two awards which are given to players on each sports team. One is given to the athlete who performs well and gives his all to the team. The second, called "Mighty In Spirit", is given to the athlete who gives strong spiritual leadership to the team. In his four years of high school, Kevin has accumulated a shelf full of "Mighty In Spirit" awards. Now Jeffrey, playing junior high basketball, has his first "Mighty In Spirit" award. I could not be more thankful that my children are leading others to be close to God.

1997

Eddie's marriage is coming apart. His wife demands he move out and so he comes to Phoenix. Eddie is extremely depressed because he wanted to work things out in his marriage. It is a very difficult time for him. I hurt very badly when I see him in pain. As we talk together, I find I can share my feelings much better than I could before the accident. Eddie is my unofficial foster son who came to live in my home when he was sixteen. I painfully learn that he has never felt my total love and acceptance as a son. The two of us grow much closer during this time. Good things can happen even during painful times.

Pastor John, from First Baptist Church, talks to me about computer software that will make a computer totally voice activated. He says quality products are now available, but are still fairly expensive. I am very interested. He provides the contact that introduces me to Dragon Dictate, a program that will enable me to run any Windows program. I eagerly purchase this program along with a laptop computer. I have found it difficult to dictate written material to my caregivers. Technology has again given me independence. Now I can prepare letters, legal documents and so much more. My sons have encouraged me to write down my philosophies and strategies in managing Little League teams. Two years ago I began to dictate this material to a caregiver, but gave up in frustration. Soon after I get my voice activated program I write a short book entitled, "Little League: The Secret to Having a Winning Season".

I change my status from inactive to active with the Arizona Bar Association and I put in another telephone line to use strictly for my law practice. Stationary is printed and I begin to accept cases. My bedroom is my law office for my limited number of cases. Practicing law gives a lift to my self-esteem. I feel like a lawyer again. I also do some fill-in teaching at Sunday school. Responsible assignments are again part of my life. I even become a member of the Board of Trustees at my church. Amazingly, I don't feel disabled any longer.

Frequently Jeffrey asks me to help him with his math homework. When he comes to me I set aside whatever I am doing. I am thankful for something just the two of us can do together. My inability to use my hands makes finding solutions to math problems and teaching math principles a challenge, but usually I am able to help him. Fortunately, I have a strong mathematics background, because Jeffrey is in advanced algebra and geometry, trig and calculus will be coming his way soon.

I get great news with regard to my lawsuit with Chrysler. At the time of the accident it was well documented that, on our model minivan, the latch on the back hatch was defective because it would open with a slight bump. In my accident, even though I was belted in, my head and shoulders broke through the back passenger side window. When the back hatch came open, the left hinge sheared off and the hatch swung around to hit me in the face, breaking my neck. A face sized dent and a hunk of my hair on the hatch prove the point. Chrysler is feeling the heat.

It's May and Alana is getting married. Her eleven cousins have come (nine all the way from the East coast) to share in this special time. She is the first of her cousins to get married and her cousins are all excited for her. Lots of planning has gone into the wedding by Marcia and especially by Alana. Alana wants everything to be perfect. It is. At the reception, when it is time for the father-daughter dance, Alana and I take the dance floor to "Butterfly Kisses", a song that wets my eyes every time I hear it played. Alana sits on my lap and we give each other butterfly kisses (eyelash kisses), as we did so long ago before each bedtime. It is a very moving experience for me. The following day I am down more than I had expected. My only daughter is gone. Alana Treat is no more. Alana Heater, Allen's Alana, is here. I am missing my Alana very much.

Marcia and I have been spending more time talking together and are growing in our relationship. However, we are never truly alone. One of my caregivers is always in the home. We have no privacy in our conversations. This is a subtle consequence of my twenty-four hour care. My caregivers are our friends, but having one of them always near is an uncomfortable way to live. I must have a caregiver available immediately if I need to have mucus suctioned from my lungs, but having someone constantly in the home can sometimes seem unbearable.

In August Kevin begins his college studies at Biola University, a Christian school in California. His leaving is very hard. Kevin is the one person always able to cheer up his mother, who otherwise seems so sad. When Alana left home she moved across town and we still see her every week. Kevin will be in California. He will be sorely missed.

Parent's weekend at Biola is in October. Priscilla encourages me to go and so Marcia, Priscilla and I drive to L.A. for my first overnight away from home since the accident. I have a terrific time. The Biola campus is beautiful and Kevin's dorm, with all his dorm buddies, is great. Kevin's intramural football team plays flag football, with Kevin its player/coach. Of course his team blows away the competition. I really love this time with Kevin! The weekend is physically very hard for me, but it has proved that I can travel.

When Kevin is home for Thanksgiving he tells us a secret. He plans to propose to Erica the following evening. Tonight he will go to her parents, when she is away, to ask their permission. Incredible! My 19-year-old son will be married next May, just one year after his sister. We adore Erica and are happy for them, but we had been expecting Kevin to be back home this summer. Instead of a summer with Kevin, we will have to be satisfied with a weekly Sunday telephone call that has become a regular occurrence since Kevin moved to California. But when Kevin and Erica are together, bubbling with excitement, their mood is contagious and we are excited too.

In December, Alana graduates with her RN degree from Grand Canyon University. Several hospitals make offers of employment to her. She chooses a day job at Thunderbird Samaritan Hospital to work in critical care. Alana has worked very hard and I am thrilled to see things going so well for her.

1998

Since late 1994 I have had a bacterial infection in my lungs that can be controlled, but not cured. It is immune to oral antibiotics. For several years it responded to an inhaled antibiotic, but now, when it flares up every few months, it must be treated with an IV antibiotic. I try to treat it as seldom as possible, because it is gradually becoming immune to the IV antibiotics. There is concern that one day it may be immune to all antibiotics. In February I wait too long to treat a flare up and I am back in the hospital with pneumonia. I'm on oxygen again, my breathing is very shallow and I feel very weak. Fortunately, I'm discharged after four days, but I continue on oxygen and IV antibiotics at home, as I recover my breathing capacity and strength. Two weeks later, when I have just begun to feel my strength returning, pneumonia strikes again. This time it is treated at home. Pneumonia makes my days very hard. Every breath is a hard pull. Shortness of breath and suffocation feelings are common. Breathing treatments every four hours and IV antibiotics every eight hours are the routines of each day. Life is a struggle. This second bout of pneumonia is especially hard. I have lost weight, I feel very weak and I believe my life will soon be over. One night when Alana is visiting, these feelings overpower me and I tell her I think I'm dying, which gets her quite upset. But God is not finished with me yet. I fully recover my strength. Oh well, I guess I'll just have to put off dying for another day.

The home health nurses who visit me provide an opportunity for a little fun. Carey, a home health nurse who comes to draw blood, needs to plug in her lap top computer to enter data. As the electrical outlets next to my bed are occupied, she asks Priscilla if it is all right to unplug the top outlet. Seeing Priscilla nod, she pulls the plug and lets it drop to the floor. I immediately pretend to gasp desperately for air. Believing the pulled plug has somehow sent me into severe respiratory distress, Carey dives to the floor to retrieve the plug and quickly restore it to the outlet. Blurting out apologies, Carey raises her eyes to see my smiling face. Her face breaks into a smile. "You got me good, David, you got me good."

My illnesses have prevented me from attending to my cases. I realize my health compromises my ability to represent my clients. In addition, I prefer to use my limited energy to do things with my family. I decide to limit my law practice to very special situations.

I have told Kevin about some of the letters I write to Kim. He wants to know why I don't write to him. He writes to me saying he misses me as his mentor. He wants letters too. As I think about what to write to him, I recall my own college days. I remember being struck by the number of students around me who were simply drifting through life, not really conscious of life-guiding goals or principles. Bringing this thought into focus for Kevin, I ask, "Why should it be any different? The media certainly tell us that there is no black or white, no right or wrong, only individual preferences." I have him consider a passage I read recently that was written by a college student:

> "My goal is that when I look back on my life I will be able to say, 'I have lived a good life, I am not ashamed of it. If I have to give it up today I will not despair because I have grappled with the roots of my

existence, I have made my life meaningful, and though I am sorry to leave the world, my conscience is clear and I leave in peace.'

How can these statements be possible, if I haven't developed a moral code as a guide in my life, to judge a 'good life' and 'good conscience' by? And if I am to accomplish my goal, it must be clear enough that I can keep it in view each day.

To walk blindly through life—with no ultimate goals or principles—is to give life away bit by bit, not realizing until it is almost all given away (and perhaps not even then), that I have forfeited the only precious thing I possessed. No wonder the despair of such a person—let it never be my despair!

I tell Kevin, "This young man is determined to 'grapple with the roots of his existence.' No easy cliché answers here. He wants to dig, and dig deep, to find where he fits in creation. He wants to thrash out black and white principles he can live by, so he can pause each day to check whether he has hit the mark. Like the apostle Paul, at the end of his life he wants to be able to say, 'I have run the race, I have kept the faith.'" I conclude my letter to Kevin with these lines: "The young man quoted above does not mention the Lord. But he knows the Lord—otherwise, how could he talk of a conscience and a moral code. I can tell you that he became closer with the Lord as he pursued his goals. This quote is from my personal journal, dated June 9, 1974."

My children are well grounded in what is important for a meaningful life. My letters, which Kevin shares with his siblings, are one more way for me to hold before them kernels of truth, separated from the chaff of falsehood that is part and parcel of the world we live in.

Kevin is married May 29th. I find that the father of the groom plays a much smaller role than the father of the bride. I don't even get to roll him down the aisle!

The date of the trial against Chrysler is approaching. Alana and Marcia are preparing plans to go to Detroit. A video has been made of me, going about a typical day, that will substitute for my personal appearance. My attorney telephones to advise me that Chrysler is finally entering into serious negotiations. Tensions are high. I cannot risk going to trial because there is always the possibility of getting nothing. I must come away with something. Five days before trial my lawyer telephones with great news: the case has been settled very favorably. My family breathes a tremendous sigh of relief. No one wanted to go to Detroit!

For four years I have not had a pressure sore, but I have a large, deep sore developing now. In early August I have surgery, which includes a skin graft. Ten days later it is obvious that part of the skin graft is going bad and another graft is made. For nineteen days I am in the hospital, flat on my back on a special mattress. It is a lonely, boring hell. I hate hospitals!

Before the accident I had fun with children. I would get down on the floor, at their level, to listen to what they had to say and to let them climb on me. I would pick them up, with their legs locked around my waist, eye to eye, to bring them to my level. They loved it when I put them on my shoulders so they were higher than the adults around them. I loved children.

Now children don't relate to me. Touch, so essential in communicating love and acceptance to young children, is now denied me. My paralyzed arms and legs and my mouthstick driven chair, make me a momentary object of curiosity, which they eye from a distance. But I can find no way to encourage them into a meaningful conversation or interaction. I miss being a part of the lives of children very much.

I have an idea for relating to my seven-year-old niece, Anna, who lives in Utah. Anna really, really likes cats. I invent a cat named Paws, who talks people-talk. Because it kind of freaks other people out to hear a cat talk people-talk, Paws has decided it is only safe to talk people-talk to me. Paws, who is a young cat, wants a human friend his own age. He writes to Anna (his huge seven towed paws have definite difficulty with Uncle David's computer keys) asking if she will be his friend, signing his letter, "One lonely people-talking cat."

My sister, Cindy, tells me Anna is very excited about her letter from Paws. "A cat that talks people-talk, Mom, and he wants to be *my* friend!" I'm not sure where this character, Paws, is going to take me, but I think I have found a way into the life of my precious niece.

Jeffrey is nearing sixteen and that means having a driver's license. Marcia and I discuss rules we feel Jeffrey should have for driving. We include a rule forbidding the car radio or CD player to be turned on for six months, another forbidding his friends under twenty-one driving his car and several other rules in our discussion. I draft our rules into a written contract for Jeffrey to sign. Jeffrey has been relentless in arguing in the past and we prepare for meeting arguments we feel he is sure to make. We tell Jeffrey we have a contract about driving we want to go over with him. Jeffrey silently reads it, glances up saying he doesn't have a problem with it, signs it and asks, "Anything else?" Marcia and I sit in stunned silence. No, there is nothing else. Jeffrey walks from the room. Something has changed with Jeffrey. It is like someone turned a switch. From then on, he doesn't fight with his mother and he doesn't argue with our rules or disciplinary punishments. He is a changed young man. I give thanks to God for answering my prayers.

1999

We celebrate Jeffrey's birthday in January and I think again on how much God has blessed me. All of my children are present at Jeffrey's birthday dinner. The conversation is lively as ever. My three boys gently tease Marcia. There is hardy laughter all around. Alana hits Eddie in the shoulder and he dutifully feigns hurt. At one point Jeffrey comes up behind Alana, pulls her to him and puts his head on her shoulder, leaning his head against hers. I sit back and watch my family. There is genuine love flowing between the members. And the protective canopy of God's love is suspended above us all.

Experiencing these times always makes me feel blessed. In this world where there is so often family strife, God is giving me the desires of my heart. God and I have had quite a number of talks about my children. Marcia and I have invested much where our hearts have been. The scene I described above is very typical, but it always makes me feel warm inside. Of course, my job as a parent is not yet finished and I plan on talking a good deal more with God about my children. Still, right now I am feeling very blessed.

I've been on the night vent for over five years and for the first time, it starts to hurt my chest after four or five hours. When I go off the vent for the rest of the night, my chest hurts more the following day because my diaphragm hasn't had enough rest. After several more months, my chest hurts terribly at my regular breath volume of 720 mls of air. Gradually, I must reduce my breath volume.

Mornings are frequently very hard. My chest hurts a lot and I struggle for enough air. Ordinarily, friendly banter is constantly on my lips, but on these mornings it hurts to talk and so I am silent. Times like these are difficult for me, but possibly even more difficult for Marcia, who must be with me and watch me struggle with life, morning after morning. I had not considered just how difficult this was for her until she asked, "Does the struggle to live ever seem too great, David? Do you ever want to just give up? It is all I can bare to watch you." But I have many good times too. I am not about to give up my struggle with life!

Jeffrey talks much more openly to Marcia and me. When I ask him what caused such a major change in his attitude in the past year he admits he was an angry kid during his junior high and early high school years. His contact with classmates who struggle with dysfunctional, ungodly families has helped him to appreciate his own parents who love him and have shared the love of God with him. Now he gently teases Marcia, causing her to smile and he frequently gives her hugs and other loving touches. Marcia has longed for her son to express love for her and she eats it up.

Eddie's life is coming together for him. He has always loved music. He has been enrolled in college in a music program for a year and is getting good grades. He performs on lead guitar in a small band. Eddie has been in my prayers and on my heart a great deal since he separated from his wife. I am relieved to see joy in his heart and smile again.

Priscilla switched to the day shift in the fall of 1998 (Chad resumed his education one and one-half years ago). She likes to get me out of the house which I'm sure is good for me. Even when I don't feel well, I find I don't feel any worse (and sometimes better) when I go somewhere. At Home Depot I pick out flowers and bushes for my yard that Priscilla gladly plants, under my direction. My gardens, which have been empty for so many years, are once again well landscaped and brimming with flowers. Frequently Priscilla schedules my doctor appointments for late morning and then talks me into stopping for Mexican food on the way home. Occasionally Marcia and I catch an afternoon movie together. I even go to a couple of Diamondback baseball games.

To my regret, I didn't see much of Jason for several years after he moved back to his father's house. But in the past year, Jason has been frequenting my home again. It feels incredibly good to have him back as part of my family.

In June, Marcia's parents are celebrating their 50th wedding anniversary. Marcia's younger brother, his wife and their three boys will be there. I very much want to be with Mom and Dad Begley on this very special occasion and I haven't seen Ron, Carol and my three nephews since Alana's wedding. It's a must for me, so I will have another 1st—a plane ride—when I travel to North Carolina. Everything goes well on the flight, but when we rent the van at the airport Priscilla manages to get two flat tires at the same time. It's a long story that allows for much kidding and laughter afterwards. Fortunately, my entourage of wife and children (including Jason) manage to take care of everything so we are on the road toward my in-laws within two hours. I have a great three days with everyone. As usual, this trip pushes me very hard physically, but it is worth it. Just seeing my family, Marcia's family and especially the cousins, playing games and enjoying each other as they interact with obvious love, does my soul good.

After the accident, I thought my ministries were gone. I was wrong. I have a team of four attendants who spend large amounts of time with me each week. They are impacted by the love they see flowing within my family. Most are unchurched until they go with me on Sunday mornings and Wednesday nights. People I see often tell me I am an inspiration to them. Previously, I couldn't understand such comments and just pushed them aside. Now I see that my presence, with my sip and puff chair, actively participating in life, may give others encouragement that they too can deal with the problems that come their way. Last year Marcia prayed with Priscilla to invite Jesus into her life. Awesome! Priscilla says that my family is a great testimony to her that there is another way to live. My ministries have changed, but they are alive and well.

In September, as Jeffrey, Eddie and Priscilla are clowning around in my room, while Marcia and I look on, a remarkable thing happens—Marcia laughs out loud. Play stops for a short moment as everyone registers what occurred. Marcia also recognizes the importance of that moment. It is a breakthrough. Thereafter, Marcia laughs regularly, sometimes hilariously. It is music to my ears.

2000

What appears to be the outline of a three and one-half inch in diameter hockey puck is easily visible just below the skin, on the left side of my tummy—my Baclofen pump. The powerful muscle relaxer, Baclofen, flows from this pump into a narrow tube, which goes to my spinal column where it drips directly onto my spinal cord. Every 29 days the pump is refilled using a very LARGE syringe. I have had the Baclofen pump five and one-half years and the battery will soon be dead. The pump must be replaced.

The pump replacement is supposed to be an overnight procedure, but I am feeling very badly the morning after surgery. My doctor decides I should stay another day in the hospital. The following morning I am still hurting. My back, shoulders and chest are in a hard spasm, as if I'm not getting any Baclofen. I tell this to my doctor, but he insists it just takes time and that I will be feeling better shortly. He elects to send me home. For two days I keep hoping my condition will improve, but it doesn't. All of the muscles in my upper back, shoulders, neck and upper chest are in extreme spasm and hard as wood. My breathing is very shallow. Every breath is a struggle. On the third morning I call my doctor's office and insist something is very wrong. An appointment is set for me the following day. That night I have an incredible headache. The pain is so great it feels like my head is about to explode. In addition, my blood pressure is running very high, so I am rushed to the ER, where my blood pressure now reads 265/160, more than twice my normal pressure. I am given medication which slowly brings my blood pressure within the normal range, but I am admitted to the hospital because there is concern it might shoot up again. The following day an imaging device shows that the tube traveling from the Baclofen pump to the spinal cord is not connected to the pump. I have not received a drop of Baclofen for six days! Surgery is scheduled immediately and the tube is reattached. It has been a tough, tough week for me. My struggle this week has reminded me of the importance of my medications. They allow me to function and move forward with my life. As I lie in my bed I give thanks such drugs are available.

Sometimes one of my nurses will fail to acknowledge me as a person when she asks my caregiver questions such as, "Did David sleep well last night? Is he hurting anywhere?" She is standing next to my bed, but it is as if I don't exist. It is a very dehumanizing experience. I could get angry, but instead I generally just interrupt by asking my caregiver whether my nurse slept well last night. That always gets the conversation going in the right direction.

The morning after my Baclofen pump is replaced, the resident neurosurgeon, Dr. Bauer, comes into my room to check on me. While standing at my bedside, he begins questioning Priscilla about how I am feeling. At the third question Priscilla says, "Why don't you ask him yourself? He can talk." The doctor looks down at me for the first time and asks me a question. Pretending to struggle very hard with my speech, I stick my tongue out of my mouth an inch and, straining very hard, blurt out, "Da-uh, Da-uh, Da-uh." Dr. Bauer looks up at Priscilla in confusion, and seeing she is laughing at me, knows the joke is on him. He turns on his heel and leaves the room. Priscilla and I can't stop laughing for several minutes. "You're bad, David. You're so bad," is all she can say. Since that morning, I have had several engaging conversations with Dr. Bauer and, to his credit, he has proved to be a good sport.

I am fifty years old in May. Marcia throws a large party for me. I receive dozens of letters from family and friends relating past experiences together. For me, it is an occasion to reflect back. I grew up in a family filled with love and with parents who modeled strong values. Marcia and I have shared a love together rarely known by marriage partners. I have children who love God and seek His ways in their lives. I have been greatly blessed and I pause to give thanks and praise to God.

As I go in and out of my home I see my grand piano. It seems to call to me. Sometimes I fancifully think it aches to feel my touch on its keys. How I long to slip onto its bench and play just one last time. At church we sing many praise songs that are new to me. As I lie in bed at night I entertain myself by playing these new melodies on the keyboard in my mind. I try out different keys, different variations. Sometimes my music rocks, other times it's a quiet prayer. I will always play the piano.

July 16 is a special day—Alana delivers my first grandchild! The four grandparents meet at the hospital with Alana and Allen. We eat pizza while Zachary Allen Heater sleeps peacefully. He is beautiful!

During the past year Jeffrey and I have become very close. On a regular basis he seeks me out to talk over issues in his life. He asks my advice on decisions facing him and always asks for prayer. His close friends are regular visitors in our home. During Jeffrey's junior high years and first year of high school he was very private in his thoughts. At that time my physical limitations prevented me from being a significant part of his life outside the home. His resistance to my questions closed me out of much of his life. I had never experienced this with one of my children. The huge change over the last year is an answer to prayer.

In September I am in court, but this time as a client. My whole family gathers with me as the judge signs the adult adoption order, legally making Eddie one with us. Marcia and I have always thought of him as our son and my children have always considered him their big brother. The adoption is a technicality, but emotionally for Eddie and us, it means very much.

My breathing capacity has continued to be a problem. Several months ago Dr. Silverthorne advised it was all right to reduce my breath volume on the vent at night, but she emphasized it should not go lower than 600 mls. I continue to try to maximize my breath volume, but my chest cavity is slowly getting smaller. By November my chest hurts terribly if the vent volume is greater than 450 to 500 mls. My body cannot sustain itself on this small amount of air unless each breath is supplemented with oxygen. I am concerned my chest cavity will continue to collapse. Dr. Silverthorne suggests I go to Craig Hospital in Colorado for an evaluation by doctors who specialize in spinal injury care. As usual, I take this very grave matter to the Lord. I have needed oxygen when I am on the vent at night for several weeks. I rarely can stay on the vent for more than a few hours before I have to go off because of chest pain. My voice is weak and wears out before the end of the day because my diaphragm is tired. If I get a serious respiratory infection in this condition I will be in real trouble. My doctor calls Craig Hospital and relays a message to me that they will be contacting me. Their call never comes. But something miraculous is happening—my chest has begun to expand. Soon my lungs accept breaths of air up to 600 mls, and sometimes more, without pain. Amazing what God can do! I don't know what my chest will do in the years ahead, but for now God has given me a reprieve and I am thankful! Pastor Norm asks me what I attribute my better breathing to. "Prayer," I tell him, "very powerful prayer."

Several times since the accident I thought I was about to die. I thought this not because I had inside information from God, but simply because I felt my health seriously declining and could not imagine life continuing. Each time God pulled me back, as if to say, "Not yet. I have more to teach you. There is more for you to do for me." One day I will cross over the line men call death. On that day I will hear the words, "Welcome home, good and faithful servant!" and I will be alive more than I have ever known. I will be greeted joyously by all the saints and especially by my older sister. Until that day, I will embrace life!

Paws is developing into quite a character. He tells Anna how her mother, as a child, broke her clarinet over Uncle David's head and broke her arm when Mike gave her an "airplane ride". Paws craves green olives, but they make him go bonkers as he runs so fast he is only a yellow blur. Paws has many adventures with his three cousins, Hiccup, Sneeze and Snort. When a large dog attacks them the cousins scatter, but Paws will not run from a dumb dog that doesn't even speak people-talk. Instead of running, he rears up on his back legs and commands, "Sit!" That poor dog's rear hits the ground and Paws walks calmly away. In a softer moment, Paws tells Anna bedtime stories. He also tells her she is more precious than diamonds or rubies to her parents and that he too, values her very highly. Anna tells Paws all about her friends and her many accomplishments. She

decorates the envelopes and draws lots of pictures
for Paws. Paws and Anna are fast friends.

2001

Zachary has been growing very fast. Nana Marcia and I enjoy babysitting for him occasionally. He flashes a large smile to anyone who comes into the room and is a joy in every way (ok, he does cry once in a while). But I can never hold my grandson. I can't get down on the floor to romp and play. When he is here, he is passed around to everyone, while I look on. Alana brings him over to me and pretends to crash him into my cheek. It is a fun game, but I long to hold and cuddle my grandson.

Sometimes I think of how things would be different with Zachary if I weren't paralyzed. I would make time for so many fun things to do with him. It is impossible not to fantasize occasionally. But mainly I think about things as they are. When he gets older he can climb up onto my lap so I can give him a ride in my chair or I

115

can read him stories, including some I have written. I will find a way into his life.

In February I have another pressure sore on my butt that requires surgery. This time, thankfully, I spend only one night in the hospital. I do not like being confined to my bed at home for the following month, but at least at home I am constantly around my family and friends. I have always loved my bright red hair, but the tender skin that comes with having red hair I don't like. After sitting upright for one to one and one-half hours, I must lay on my side for thirty minutes. If I try to cheat on this my skin soon breaks down and I am headed for surgery again. I have had six surgeries on my butt and I am trying hard to avoid having a seventh.

Every time I see a new doctor I must fill out a form listing dozens of diseases and conditions and requesting that I check those that apply to me. I always come away from completing one of these forms feeling that I'm in pretty good shape. Things could be a lot worse!

Jeffrey graduates from high school in May. We hold an all day reception for him at our home. The following evening Jeffrey has a big graduation party with his high school friends around our pool. In a few days we're off to Los Angeles to see Kevin graduate with a degree in mathematics and a minor in Bible (Erica graduated the previous

December). I must return to Phoenix after his graduation ceremony, but Marcia stays on a few days to see him sworn in as a Second Lieutenant in the Air Force. It has been a whirlwind two weeks for me.

My children are doing well. Eddie has continued with his schooling and in two years he will graduate from Grand Canyon University with a degree in music education. Alana has cut her work back to one day a week since Zachary's birth. She enjoys her new role as a mother very much. Kevin and Erica are awaiting orders to go to Vandenberg Air Force Base for Kevin's training as a missileer. They are cautiously excited about becoming part of the Air Force "family". In the fall Jeffrey will move to Flagstaff to begin college at Northern Arizona University. Jason will graduate in two years with a degree in political science and intends to then apply to law school. My children are growing up. All are firm in their faith.

Marcia's attitude toward life has changed. Spontaneous emotions flow from her easily. She no longer believes all the good times are behind her. Early this year Marcia organized, and began leading, a Thursday night women's Bible study group. Several months ago she and another woman began team teaching a Sunday school class. It has been almost eight years since the

117

accident. Marcia has always had strong abilities in teaching and counseling. She is now putting these abilities to work with great power, as she did before the accident. Marcia's doctors have told me many times that it takes years for new pathways to be established in the brain to make up for those lost in the accident. I have certainly witnessed positive changes each year with Marcia.

Marcia and I have continued to grow together. We are a great crossword puzzle team! We pray together for others and especially for our children. We again express love for each other and my life burns brighter for it.

I am excited! I have just received notice I have been selected to be a torchbearer for the 2002 winter Olympics in Salt Lake City. I knew my niece, sister and mother had nominated me, but there were several hundred thousands of nominations across the country. I did not expect to be one of those selected. Now I will carry the Olympic torch for a short distance through Phoenix in January. Unbelievable!

Marcia and I were leaders with the junior and senior high youth at church before the accident. Our inability to participate after the accident left a vacuum of leadership the youth pastor found difficult to fill. It has been hard for me to see the youth program struggle. Early this year two people eager to help with the youth stepped forward: Priscilla and a former caregiver of mine, Marc. I am very humbled. God is still teaching me.

David A. Treat

Concluding Remarks (July 2001)

My family has been blanketed with prayer since the beginning. Prayer chains across the country were established within hours after the accident. My church congregation, family and friends continue to pray for us on a regular basis. Many miracles have occurred along the way, the greatest of which is Marcia's incredible recovery. The power of prayer is great!

Marcia has said many times that before the accident she thought she was indispensable in raising our children. Both of us now realize that God loves our children even more than we do. When we were not there, God provided. Before the accident we knew in our head that God is faithful. Now this knowledge is emblazoned on our hearts. God *is* faithful!

Shortly after the accident I felt a bowling ball had struck my family taking Marcia and me out with one blow. My faith wavered, but God did not waver. He caught me and my family up in his arms and carried us until we could walk again. I felt my family had been crushed. How wrong I was! My family was being made strong, powerful and with a capacity to love greater than I could have ever imagined. One of my prayers for my children has always been that they would be strong in their knowledge and faith in God. My children are warriors for God. Their faith and knowledge of the Lord surpasses what I would have thought possible. I am truly blessed!

Most of us will, at some point in our life, experience tough times when our life seems to be coming apart. "Going through the fire," is a thought that comes with fear and trembling. But the words in James 1:1-4 ring true—the fires of life do build endurance; they do make us complete. Nevertheless, it is a rare Christian who welcomes the passages of fire that come to him. Fires rage hot and they leave scars. I have shared my personal fire-going so that you may be encouraged, and know that when the fires rage about you, God will be with you and bless you along the way. My prayers go with you.

David A. Treat

For Marcia

We came together in our youth.
Together we formed a cradle of love about us.
Three children came to us
And our cradle of love grew larger.
A fourth child was sent by God.
Again our cradle of love was enlarged.
For 22 years we lived and loved together.
And the Lord God watched over us.

Then our cradle of love was ripped apart.
Within only a few moments
      our lives were forever changed.
Hospitals, doctors, paralysis, interminable
      separations.
Permanent changes to our minds and bodies.
We had become different persons.
And I was lost from you!
Still the Lord God watched over us.

Does he love me as I am or only as I was?
Does he even have an inkling of who I am?
How can she love me, paralyzed and numb,
A mere whisper of the man I once was?
Frightening questions that shout for an answer.
Oh God! My spirit is poured out.
The pain is too great—too great.
And the Lord God watched over us.

122

Unending tears, resisting what is,
     yearning for what can never be.
A year and more has come and gone.
But slowly, ponderously slowly,
We begin to discover each other again
Two steps forward, one and one-half steps back,
The process has begun.
Can it be—may we even dare to hope—
Our cradle of love is coming together again?
And the Lord God watches over us.

         David A. Treat
         September 1, 1995

Epilogue (June 2003)

Paws' letters to Anna have been so popular with children that I have now used them to create a series of illustrated children's books. They include such titles as *The Adventures Of Paws The People-Talking Cat*, *Paws And His Cousins*, *Paws Tells Bedtime Stories*, *Paws Goes Snowboarding*, *Paws And Mr. Emery* and others. I expect the first title to be available by late 2003, with other titles to follow every three to six months.

Publication of these books will give me the opportunity to go into public libraries for "story time" with children. I have found a way to interact with children after all!

Of course, Paws and Anna remain great friends and although Anna has guessed Paws' identity, she insists, "Paws, you are a very special cat. You will always be Paws." And so Paws' letters continue.

About the Author

David Treat is a native of Phoenix, Arizona where he and his wife of 31 years, Marcia, have raised their four children. He graduated from law school at the University of Arizona in 1977. In 1993 his family was involved in a serious auto accident leaving him a quadriplegic on a vent and his wife with a very significant brain injury. David's physical, emotional and spiritual journey following this accident provides the backdrop for *Going Through The Fire, Developing A Faith That Perseveres.*

Made in the USA
San Bernardino, CA
22 August 2018